Praise

Out of the Bronx

"Irene Sardanis writes with compulsion, ferocity, and immediacy of a wrongly imprisoned person, unexpectedly and surprisingly set free - which, of course, she is: a prisoner of time, place, family, gender, culture, religion and self."
—MARK GREENSIDE, author of *I Saw a Man Hit His Wife* and *I'll Never Be French (no matter what I do)*

"*Out of the Bronx* is a spellbinding tale of how to survive the worst kind of childhood and thrive in later life. Author Irene Sardanis, the daughter of Greek immigrants, takes readers on her healing journey, one that began with a violent mother and often absent, alcoholic father. Richly compassionate, Ms. Sardanis eventually built a career as a therapist and found the love of her life. Along the way, she discovered a hard-won surprise, compassion for her mother and father. The memoir is a haunting reminder of the era when few persons thought of intervening when a young person was abused, and before anyone heard of child protective services. Whether one's parents arrived from another place recently or long ago, *Out of the Bronx*, offers considerable inspiration for all readers."
—KRISTINE MIETZNER, Contributor, *Your Life is a Trip*

"Irene Sardanis's writing is as spunky as she is, and we cheer for her as she negotiates her way from being an abused child to a teenager who tries to outwit her mother to an adult who survived two abusive marriages, got her doctorate in psychology, worked as a therapist, and found love. Her insight, understanding, and humor are there in her memoir for the reader to experience. This book could be depressing. Instead, it's an inspiration."

—KAREN LEE PLISKIN, PhD, anthropologist,
author of *Silent Boundaries*

"How we come through our childhood is a mystery. Even with dynamics laid out plainly as Irene Sardanis does in her memoir, her voice is so utterly clear you can see her world. She says, 'I knew I could never tell anyone.' Yet she bravely tells us her story. Read *Out of the Bronx* and you may be honored with a glimpse of the mystery."

—CLIVE MATSON, author of *Hello, Paradise. Paradise,
Goodbye.* and *Let the Crazy Child Write*

Out

of the

Bronx

A MEMOIR

Irene Sardanis, Ph.D.

SHE WRITES PRESS

Published May 2019
Printed in the United States of America
Print ISBN: 978-1-63152-539-1
E-ISBN: 978-1-63152-540-7
Library of Congress Control Number: 2018968512

For information, address:
She Writes Press
1569 Solano Ave #546
Berkeley, CA 94707

Interior design by Tabitha Lahr

She Writes Press is a division of SparkPoint Studio, LLC.

Names and identifying characteristics have been changed to protect the privacy of certain individuals.

For Ms. B.

And Still I Rise

—Dr. Maya Angelou

Contents

Introduction

I never expected to write a book about my past. Happily, I took writing classes, went to conferences, and hid behind a false facade. I could write anything I wanted. No one would read it. No one would find out what happened to me. Everything was fine. I was fine.

Three years ago my therapist suggested, "You've done some good work in your life. When you go to New York for the annual Greek Easter, why don't you find Miss Jackson, the therapist you saw when you were sixteen, and thank her?"

What a great idea. I quickly googled her name and sadly learned that she'd passed away several years earlier. *Oh no*, I thought. I wanted to see her again. I grieved her more than my own mother. I wanted to see her, tell her she saved my life, tell her how much she meant to me and that I loved her.

No more denial. I knew I had to write my memoir, to dedicate it to her, to thank her for everything she gave me: her time, her patience, and her wisdom. If my writing journey offers hope to at least one other person who came from an immigrant family and suffered, then I must write it. I want to say to that person, "Please read my story and know you are not alone. Reach out and ask for help, even when you don't believe you'll get it. Don't ever give up."

In the 1950s, there was no Child Protective Services. I remember being on the train in New York and seeing a sign: Society for the Prevention of Cruelty to Animals. *What about children?* I wondered. *What about me?*

Years ago, when first I faced my mother on the page, I heard her warning voice in my head: *You better not tell anyone what happened. Don't you dare say a word. If you do, I'll curse you from my grave.*

At first, I felt afraid; then the revelation. *Too late, Ma*, I said, *I'm going to write the truth and you can't stop me.*

I took writing classes with Elizabeth Fishel, Charlotte Cook, Mark Greenside, Clive Matson, and Louise Dunbar. I attended writing seminars with Natalie Goldberg and Laura Davis. Writing conferences took me to many cities. I wanted to learn to craft my story well.

There's something amazing about being at a conference with a group of strangers who grow close through sharing their writing. This is my tribe; these people are all writers. Being together gives us courage to bleed on the page and tell our stories.

I hired a writing coach, Charlotte Cook, who put my feet to the fire. She made me write things I didn't want to write. Inside I'd say to myself, *I don't want to do it. I won't do it.* I rebelled.

We taped our sessions. I went home and listened to what she said, and I was able to write some of the best parts of the memoir, like "Carmen Miranda" and "When My Mother Cooked."

When Charlotte left the area, I found a new coach, Kira Allen. Kira said there was a missing part to the memoir: the part of how I came to California from New York.

This was a painful part of my life, and I didn't want to write about it. There was a lot of shame I didn't want to revisit. I didn't want anyone to know about that part of my story.

"You can do it," she said. "Don't think about sequence or grammar. Just write what you remember."

I could hardly look at the first draft of "Sotiris." I took the rough writing to a class that gave insightful feedback. I wrote, rewrote, and revised it until my coach said, "Enough." I couldn't believe that I wanted to keep going with a piece I could hardly touch initially.

Two years ago I attended a writing conference in Berkeley, "The Magic of Memoir," led by Linda Joy Myers and Brooke Warner. They invited attendees to contribute a personal essay about their process of writing, to share the obstacles, and also discussed the incentives for an anthology. I submitted my story of how initially I loved hating my mother, and how my writing exploring her life transformed mine.

I learned there were over two hundred responses to their invitation, and only forty were accepted. It was a humbling moment when I learned I was one of the forty.

It's been a long journey from New York to California and an even longer one from my first published piece, "The Tree," in the *Psychotherapy Networker*. I want to buy a T-shirt that says "I survived the Bronx and my crazy Greek family."

———

I survived to write my story. You can too.

1. THE GREEK FESTIVAL

I'm on a mission. The day I've been waiting for all year has arrived: the Greek Festival. All I feel this Friday morning in May is my stomach growling, famished for all the Greek food waiting for me. *Feed me*, my stomach says.

This is what I live for. My running shoes are on, in preparation for to fill my great hunger for all things Greek: food, music, and especially the sweet loving *yia-yias*, the grandmothers from the church. They're the ones I secretly need the most. I look for the kind, loving, welcoming old ladies who will see me and want to invite me home for dinner. How I long for that warmth in my life. It's been absent for such a long time. My mother suffered from depression and had little energy for parenting or cooking. Today, no one must stand in the way of my quest. I leave my husband behind. He knows I'll share my bounty with him later. I'm ready to go.

Feed me, my stomach says. I could eat a cow.

I'm in Old Dependable, my Honda, hands on the plastic steering wheel, pulling out of my driveway and ready to go. My foot is heavy on the pedal, prepared to push my old car to move fast on the first day of the festival.

Once I pass through the entrance to that sacred space, every tempting delicacy calls to me. No one is there but me and my quest for the traditional food. All people disappear. I ignore everyone around me. I go into another zone of being. I change into a person most people would not recognize. I emerge as Irene, the Greek. I surrender to that core part of me, the part that dives into my culture and embraces all of it.

An inner hunger draws me to the festival. Greek food stimulates the primitive need for nourishment and gratification inside. The culture provides the fulfillment for me to find something missing in my life: family. Here, I yearn for another tribe to welcome, embrace, and invite me into their circle. I look for connection. I find it through the old Greek women who sense my need to belong.

I head for the large dining room. Long lines of men and women wait in front of me to order their food. People at tables enjoy their lunch as strolling musicians sing to them.

A woman stands behind me in line. Around forty, blond, slender, and tall, she wears an attractive beige pantsuit; and here I am in my grungy, gray sweatpants and stained T-shirt. Our goal may be the same, but the way to get there is different.

She attempts to engage me in conversation.

"Is this your first time at the Greek Festival?" she asks.

I don't respond. I pretend not to hear her. In my mind, I say to her, *Please, lady, don't speak to me. I'm on a mission. I'm not another customer in line at any old festival. I am a prodigal child coming home to my family.*

Just ahead of me are two tables of hot trays of food. The aroma drives me crazy. Smells of garlic, onion, and oregano surround the rows of lamb shanks with tomato sauce and green beans. I size up my dinner menu for the night: pastitsio, moussaka, *dolmathakia*, and *keftethes*. The first two items are pasta and eggplant casseroles with a béchamel sauce; the third is a stuffed grapevine leaf rice roll covered with a tangy egg-lemon sauce; the fourth is meatballs in tomato sauce. My hands grip the shopping bags. I want everything.

I control the impulse to dive behind the counter and scoop my hand into all the temptations before me. I want to grab a *dolma* and a hunk of a *pastitsio* with béchamel sauce dripping over me, devour all of them, and lick my fingers in ecstasy. This is not just Greek food for me. It's love in my mouth.

I scan the servers—a man in his forties, a woman in her sixties, and then the one I've been looking for: a woman in her eighties, gray hair, a worn apron around her waist, warm brown eyes. Bingo. I found her, one of the *yia-yia*s. My eyes rest on her kind face, comforted by her presence. Her hair is pulled back in a bun. The wrinkles on her face tell me she's had a hard life. In my imagination, she has several children and grandchildren who adore her. How I wish I were one of them. Could she adopt another child? Me? I look at her eyes and then it hits me. Once again, there's no escape from that familiar feeling, my mother-hunger: the constant ever-present yearning for a loving mother. Here I am still looking for the idealized one. I've searched for her everywhere.

In Greek, I say to her, "The biggest piece of everything please."

She comes close to me, explores my face, and waves the people behind me to go around to another server. The *yia-yia* asks me, "*Pinas, paithi mou*" (Are you hungry, my child)? How did she sense that so quickly?

I lower my eyes. "Yes," I reply, "I'm hungry." Little does she know just how starved I am, not only for food but for a deep longing, something absent from my early life. Her withered hand picks up a dolma from a tray, slips it on a napkin and hands it to me. "*Parto, paithi mou*" (Take it, my child), she says. There's an unspoken understanding between us. She knows me. I eat the dolma in one bite. The *yia-yia* looks at me and laughs. "Of course I'll give you the largest piece of everything," she says and grins. "And for you, the very best piece. Show me what you'd like." All this is said in Greek, of course.

I point to the biggest pieces in the tray. "No, not the one at the end," I say. "Give me that big one in the middle." She uses a spatula and scoops up the large piece of moussaka into a container.

For a brief moment, there's an invisible link between us, an unspoken awareness that I'm not just another stranger in line. I'm the real deal, someone who knows and appreciates the ingredients in every dish, respecting the effort she undoubtedly put into making them with her own hands. She knows I am a Greek. We are connected.

She fills the square container with pieces of everything I ask for. The lamb shank with rice will be our dinner entrée and the other dishes will be our appetizers. I watch the loving *yia-yia* as she puts all the food in a box, closes it, and gives me the container. I take it from her with both hands. I don't want to drop it.

"*Na'se kala*" (Be well), she says. "*Eheis tin efhi mou*" (You have my blessing). Words I wish I'd heard from my own mother.

"*Yiasou, Yia-Yia,*" I say. "*Efharisto poli.*" Thank you, Grandmother. My bag of food is full with gratitude. I pay at the register, turn, and wave goodbye to the *yia-yia*. Now, onward to the other booths.

To the left outside the dining hall there's an outdoor stall with *spanakopita* and *tiropita*. These are spinach-and-feta-cheese-filled phyllo dough triangles the size of my hand, which are appetizers to the main meal. Warm from an oven, these morsels are addictive. Once you have a taste, you want another. I purchase two of each and leave. I may eat one on the way home.

My empty bags are almost full.

Everywhere are throngs of people—schoolchildren, men, and women. The lady who stood behind me I see is now purchasing two white-and-blue embroidered skirts, handmade from some island in Greece. Others line up to buy jewelry and Greek CDs.

The scene. In my mother's village, her view was the Aegean Sea and, off in the distance, a Turkish island. Mine is of the Bay Area and, from a distance, the outline of San Francisco.

Pangs of hunger hit my belly. I head for the booth with the lamb gyros. The gyro is one of those fast foods, a wrap filled with thin slices of lamb and a secret yogurt sauce. The server prepares a gyro for me. I resist eating it right there. I'll gobble it when I get home.

More people push and shove behind me like I'm back in Manhattan's Times Square on New Year's Eve. Everyone wants one of those gyros in their mouth, like Nathan's hot dogs.

The last stop at the festival is my favorite one: the pastry room. This is where every sweet Greek delicacy is displayed. There are *kourabiethes*, butter cookies covered with powdered sugar, and *finikia* or *melomacarona*, a honey-drenched cookie my mother used to make. The other desserts, like baklava, hold no interest for me—too sweet. Just give me the *galatobouriko*, a honey-custard-filled phyllo dough, delicately sweetened, that goes straight into the mouth, just slipping in there past my tongue with no effort whatsoever. That's the absolutely best dessert on earth.

Outside the pastry room is another cubicle with other sweets—*loukoumathes*, fried doughnut holes covered with cinnamon, honey, and nuts. They're perfect with a morning cup of coffee.

My once empty bags are now full.

Yet there's one last thing I need to do. I am drawn to the live music.

Musicians on a stage play bouzoukis, guitars, and a clarinet. The men sit on wooden chairs, glasses of ouzo at their feet. One of the guys has a cigarette dangling from his mouth. They all play imported instruments. Suddenly a flood of memories comes to me of my father dancing the *Zeibekiko*, solo, a glass of booze in one hand, snapping the fingers of the other. He moved around the room, eyes closed as if in a trance as he jumped up and smacked his thighs. "*Opa!*" he'd say. "*Opa!*"

Music starts. A circle of men and women get up to join hands. They move with gusto and dance the *Kalamatiano*, a traditional line dance. The lead dancer twirls a handkerchief, and leaps and spins around. I place my bags on a chair off to the side and grab someone's hand to join in. No invitation necessary. I just dive into the dance. My feet remember the steps. This is not Oakland. I'm in another country. I'm now in Greece, my mother's country, with the cousins and aunts from the island of Lesbos, all of us dancing in harmony, all of us crazy, happy Greeks.

My mother's village was her extended family. At the festival, the Greeks are mine. The dancers squeeze my hand, their connection with me flowing through their fingers, all this love coming through their unstoppable spirit. "*Opa, opa, opa!*" they say as we move together to the music. *Opa!* Hooray!

Time for me to exit.

I can leave now.

I've filled my empty.

2. MY IMMIGRANT PARENTS

We had to guess her age. My mother was born on the island of Lesbos, the eldest of six—three sisters and three brothers. A midwife birthed her, and there is no known birth certificate. As the eldest in the family, responsibility rested on her shoulders when her parents were away gathering olives from their groves. She was taken out of school at an early age.

Although she resented being given the burden of disciplinarian, cook, and housekeeper for her siblings, she never complained to her parents. Like many women who come from a small village, she had no voice to express her feelings. My mother missed out on a childhood. That loss was passed on to all her children, especially me.

She never learned to read or write, and envied her sisters who left for school each day. My mother would tell me stories of how she wept with envy one day when her sister came home with a pencil. She wanted to go to school too, to be free to go out and play as her sisters and other children did. She took her anger out on her sisters. As a female in a Greek household, it was understood that no one ever questioned parental authority. It was ingrained at an early age to listen and obey.

Besides gathering olives from the groves, my grandfather took off on ships that came to port. When he returned home after a few months, my grandmother often became pregnant. My mother would cry with powerless rage when she saw another baby was on its way. She knew it would be her responsibility to raise the child.

The village was an extended family for my mother. She knew everyone—the grandmothers, the priests, and the shopkeepers—and they knew her. The view from her kitchen window was of the Aegean Sea and, off in the distance, Turkey. Years later, I asked my mother if she ever got angry with her parents and expressed her frustration dealing with the heavy burden of raising her siblings. "Never," she said. "My parents were saints." End of conversation.

With no work available, it was a rite of passage for young men to set out for jobs on boats in the harbor. Her brother Philip signed up on one of them and went off to sea.

It was on one of the cargo ships that Philip met Costa, another Greek from a town close to Athens. They hit it off and became drinking buddies. Philip told Costa he had three sisters that needed to be married off. It is the custom in the Greek culture that the eldest sister marries before the others, so my mother, Maria, was chosen for Costa. When Philip's ship docked in New York, wrote to his mother, "Send Maria to New York. I found a husband for her."

Plans were made for my mother to leave the village and go to Athens where she would stay with Costa's brother and family until her visa arrived to board a ship to New York so she could marry my father. She didn't want to go. How could she leave her village where she knew everyone to go to a foreign country? How could she leave to marry a stranger, even though his photograph showed a handsome man with sparkling brown eyes and a beaming smile? Her sisters needed her to marry so they could find Greek men and go to America too. She had mixed emotions as she prepared for her journey.

It took three days by donkey to get to the port of Mytilene. Maria's whole family came to see her off. They all knew she might never return to the village again. It was a sorrowful day when everyone placed all her things into a sheet, tied it with a knot, and put her on the boat to Athens. At the relatives' home, she was exhausted both physically and emotionally. Maria slept most of the time. She was sad and fearful to leave her family and relatives to marry a stranger she'd never met. Several weeks later her visa arrived. Maria left Greece on June 10, 1922, on the SS *King Alexander.*

The port of departure was Piraeus, where passengers boarded the ship to New York. She was terrified. My mother had never left her village, and now she was to be on a ship with strangers. The boat carried 250 passengers, mostly young women who were also betrothed to men in America. The journey took twenty-two days over choppy seas, and she was seasick most of the trip. However, the friends she made among the other women were a comfort to her. These women shared similar sorrows of being uprooted from their families and homes. On the boat, close friendships were formed that endured long after they were settled in New York. These women were more than acquaintances; they became a close extended family.

Everyone was excited when they saw the Statue of Liberty. After the ordeal on sea, at last the voyage was over. They arrived on July 2, 1922, and were taken to Ellis Island to process paperwork before being permitted to enter New

York and meet their future husbands. Her brother Phillip had arranged my parents' marriage by proxy prior to July 6, 1922.

Two people could not have been more opposite: my mother, an illiterate peasant from a small village, and my father, a worldly traveler.

My father was born in 1894 in the northern region of Greece, in the village of Arcadia. When he was two, his father died suddenly, leaving his mother a widow with two sons and no one to provide for them. Matchmakers arranged for her to marry a widower with five sons. After their marriage, they had two more sons. Unfortunately, the stepfather was cruel. He did not like the boy who was to become my father and singled him out for abuse. The man pressured his wife to have my father and his younger brother sent to a paternal aunt in Athens. The boys took their belongings on a train to Athens, which was the last time my father saw his mother. He never forgave her for that rejection.

The aunt accepted both boys but took a special liking to my father. She liked to cook and took my father with her to the local farmers' markets. He'd observe as she selected the firm tomatoes, eggplants, green peppers, and onions. In her kitchen he helped his aunt put the vegetables together to make a meal. School held no interest for him. Maybe he could be a cook on a boat. At sixteen he went to the harbor to find work on a ship. One captain tossed him off the ship, "Come back in another year. You're too young," he said.

My father persisted, asking for any job on the docks. Finally he was hired to work on a cargo ship where he was given odd jobs—lifting and moving crates, helping other seamen scrub the deck and tie ropes, and assisting the kitchen staff. He loved the sea and traveling to different ports.

Whenever the ship anchored, he sought women for pleasure. He was not very tall, but he had an inviting smile and charm that women liked. He would brag to others about bedding his many conquests in each port. Husbands would chase him with knives, he would say, laughing, as he ran like hell for the boat and the next port.

Preparations were made for my parents to meet and marry in New York. What a catastrophe! My father did not want to marry anyone. He loved freedom and the single life. He certainly would not have chosen my mother, a peasant woman, plain in appearance and devoutly religious. He looked for a way out of the marriage, but he had given his word. He was trapped.

There is a Greek expression *"lathie ke xithie"* (oil and vinegar), which describes my parents perfectly. They did not mix. Their interests and values were not the same. My mother valued family, religion, and her home. My father liked to drink, talk politics, and party with others. I would describe them as Maria, the saint, and Zorba, the Greek. Two total opposites.

On my mother's honeymoon, that first night in bed with my father was a frightening one. She knew nothing about sex. Things like that were never discussed in her home. As a girl from a small village, she only knew it was a wife's duty to satisfy her husband. My father took her to a cheap hotel room in downtown Manhattan where she scratched all night from the bedbugs. She was a virgin. Sex for the first time was painful and she bled on the sheets.

My parents moved to a poor neighborhood in the Bronx where there were no trees. Tall gray tenement buildings lined the streets. In the apartments were Negroes, Italians, some Greeks, and many Puerto Ricans. My mother feared everyone and trusted no one. Except to shop for food, she rarely left the apartment. She missed her family, the familiar people in her village, the Aegean Sea outside her door. In her bedroom she made an altar of religious icons of Christ, Mary, and the baby Jesus. There on her knees, she prayed.

My father found work as a house painter, but work was sporadic. The pay he earned was spent on clothes for himself, alcohol, and women. My parents fought about money. Often. She'd shout at him, "The rent. The rent. Where is the money for the rent?" He slapped her around, and she threw curses at him as he bolted out the door.

She gave birth to her first child—a daughter they named Titsa, or Tina to Americans. A year later a son was born— William, or Billy. By this time, my father was out most nights drinking, gambling, and bedding other women. My parents bickered frequently about money, his drinking and gambling his paycheck away. My mother regretted her marriage but truly loved my father. What could she do? She had no means to return to Greece. "*Eitane ei tichie mou*," she would say. (He was my fate, my destiny.)

My mother had two more unwanted children—two daughters. My father wanted her to abort them both, but my mother felt God would punish her and refused. By the time I was born, the last of four, my parents' marriage was in shambles. It was never a strong relationship. She was never a happy woman; now she became a bitter one.

As the youngest child, I was an attention seeker. I followed my father around everywhere. I adored him. He favored me and ignored my mother. Rejected by my father, my mother sought a channel for her misery. She found it in me.

3. THE DOLL

One Christmas, in 1938 when I was five, my godparents came to visit. This was a rare occasion. As a couple, my godparents were similar to my own parents in this way: they were two people who should never have married. My godmother was a tall, thin woman who wore her black hair in a tight bun at the nape of her neck. Her lined face was gaunt and drawn. She talked to herself, mumbling incoherently. Her husband, Philip, was my father's best friend and my maternal uncle; he had short, dark, wavy hair and a potbelly. He always had a glass of whiskey in his hand. When we'd visit him in Brooklyn, the first place we went was the saloon on the corner where we'd find him on a bar stool with his arm around a young woman next to him, tossing down a beer.

Philip carried a huge, white, rectangular box with a red ribbon into our living room and placed it in my lap. "This is for you," he said. "Merry Christmas." Giddy with a five-year-old's anticipation, I opened my Christmas gift. There she was: a doll—a big, beautiful doll. She looked just like Shirley Temple with blond curls and blue eyes that opened and shut. Underneath her pink dress, she had white lace panties, and she was mine. I held her close in my arms and loved her instantly.

My mother only allowed me to play with the doll on brief special occasions that she'd designate, like when company came over. Then she'd get the doll out and let me play with it. I can only imagine what was in my mother's mind. I wonder if she saw this gift as too nice and new to have it available for my everyday use. Maybe my mother thought I wouldn't take care of it. Whenever she'd put the doll in my arms, I never wanted to let it go. I hugged my dolly close, rocked her, danced with her, talked to her, and kissed her face. After I'd play with her for a while, my mother would take the doll from me and hide it. I tried to watch where she'd put it so I could find the doll on my own when she was away. But I never could climb high enough on the chair to reach the shelf and get the box.

Whenever those special occasions occurred, my mother took my doll down from the tall shelf in the living room. I could hardly wait to have her back in my arms. The doll was big, almost as tall as I was. To me she was more than a doll; she was my playmate. "Would you like a cookie?" I'd ask my dolly. Then I would pretend to feed her. We'd walk around the apartment as I held her small hand. When my mother took her from my arms, I would kiss her face. I loved her so much.

The following Christmas, one of my mother's women friends, Kiria Pelagia, came to visit, bringing along her daughter who was about my age, a child who never spoke. The girl just sat next to her mother and looked at me. Like my mother, this was a woman who had an unhappy marriage. This plain-looking, short, thin woman with a pale face had sad, drooping lines at both corners of her mouth. She wore a drab gray dress with a black wool sweater that she nervously picked at. My mother enjoyed being with other women who shared sorrowful lives.

The woman sat in the kitchen at our chipped, white porcelain kitchen table while my mother made coffee.

"Men!" my mother spat out, standing at the stove, wiping her hands on her soiled apron. "Who needs them? They are miserable dogs who destroy our lives." I knew she was referring to my absent father, who was rarely around.

The women nodded in agreement, both of them adding fuel to the fire, cursing the irresponsible men in their lives. "To hell with them all," my mother said as she poured the dark Turkish coffee into small cups. She opened a round canister from the kitchen cabinet and put out some *koulourakia*, traditional Greek cookies, on a plate.

As this was a special occasion, my mother got up from the table, brought my doll from its hiding place, and gave her to me. I held her while the other girl watched.

"Why don't you two play together?" my mother said. All I wanted was to hold my doll, never mind the girl, but I was trained to do as I was told, so we sat on the floor facing each other. I held onto my doll, unwilling to share. My mother's attention shifted from me to the woman just as she put her head down on the table and began to cry, overcome with emotion and hardly able to speak. My mother leaned over and touched her thin arm with concern. "What did he do to you?" she asked eagerly. "You can tell me."

The woman wiped her eyes with the sleeve of her sweater. "He got drunk, beat me, and left the house. Look at the bruises he left on my arms," she said, lifting her sweater to show the purple marks. "I haven't seen him since. He left no money, and I don't know how we're going to go on." The woman covered her face and continued to weep. My mother took her hand to offer comfort and gave the woman a handkerchief from her torn apron pocket. The woman's daughter just sat at her feet and looked up at her mother. "Go and play," the woman said, as she gently pushed her daughter closer to me. I didn't want to play with this girl, no matter what her mother said. I wished they'd both leave. My heart flooded with anxiety; I had an intuitive sense of what was coming next.

My mother came over and bent down beside me. "This little girl didn't get any gifts at all for Christmas. Isn't that sad?" she asked. "I know you want to give her your doll, don't you?" She didn't wait for an answer, but removed my small fingers one by one from the doll and gave it to the girl. I felt overwhelming powerless fury toward my mother, who dared to take my adored doll and give her away to this girl.

I remember my mother telling me later she'd felt sorry for the woman's situation and wanted to show some generosity toward her. After all, she had no money to give this woman. Instead my mother forced me to part with something of mine. She liked to impress others with her goodness so she could justify her righteous behavior. "These people were poor," she'd say, as if we weren't. "It was the Christian thing to do."

It pained me that I stifled my voice to speak out. If I did, I would have let out a bloodcurdling scream they'd have heard down the block. "No! No! No! It's mine! Give me back my dolly!" I'd be crying my eyes out with sorrow and despair. Sadly, I had no voice then.

I wish I could say sometime later that I was given other dolls to play with, but that's not true. There were no other dolls in my young life. The Shirley Temple doll was my only one. For a short while, I remembered how good it felt to hold her in my arms. I still miss her.

4. THE SNOWSUIT

It was an early winter evening in our Bronx tenement apartment. I was five years old and sat on a closed toilet seat in my pajamas as I watched my father shave. He wore a faded flannel bathrobe. He moved a long razor back and forth rhythmically on a brown leather strap as he carefully lathered and slowly shaved his handsome face. He was not tall, but his eyes were a warm, dark brown like his thick hair. He was the most important person in my life. I adored my father.

Without a word spoken, I knew he was going out alone to party. I didn't want him to leave. *Please stay*, I said inside. He teased me, put shaving cream on my nose. The rest of the house was deadly silent. In the living room, my mother lay on the couch. She was not resting. She was alert. My oldest sister and brother were away somewhere.

Our small apartment was cold and quiet. I could hear the Big Ben clock *tick-tocking* in the bedroom. My middle sister, Dora, was outside playing, wearing the new blue snowsuit bought by her wealthy godparents. My brown snowsuit was torn at the knees. It was understood that my sister and I would share the new snowsuit. This was how I knew we were poor. There was not enough money to buy two snowsuits. The new one was to be shared. All my clothes were hand-me-downs from my sisters or given to us by relatives.

My father splashed Old Spice aftershave on his face. He laughed and put some on mine too. I loved the smell of it. He threw a towel around his neck and smiled at his image in the bathroom mirror.

I followed my father as he walked to the bedroom. As he opened a wooden closet, I saw a row of colorful ties. He selected one, took off his bathrobe, put on a crisp, white shirt, and knotted the red striped tie. He hummed as he put on his dark pants and zipped up his fly. He put on his dark jacket. He knew he looked good. The shoes he selected were black, pointed-toed patent leather. He sat on the bed as he pulled on socks and then put on the shiny new shoes. He stood up and he was ready to go out.

The front door opened. My sister slammed the door shut and came in out of the cold winter weather wearing the new blue snowsuit. I ran after her into the living room.

"Now it's my turn to wear the snowsuit," I said.

"No," she said defiantly. "It's mine." She stuck out her tongue at me. She would not share the suit.

My mother said nothing, ignoring our bickering, and just lay stiffly there on the couch. She was not sleeping. Her lips were tight. She looked angry, unaware of me and my sister. She was in her own world.

I ran to the bedroom where my father was lacing up his fancy shoes.

"Pa," I said whining. "Dora won't take off the snowsuit. I want to wear it and go down to play."

"She won't take it off, eh?" he said. "We'll see about that."

He stomped into the hallway leading to the living room, those shiny, black shoes *clip-clopping* on the wooden floor. He pointed at my sister. "Take off the snowsuit right now and share it with your little sister."

"No," my sister replied. "It's mine. I don't want to take it off."

My father went over and whacked her across the face.

My sister cried out, "It's mine. The snowsuit is mine. She can't have it!"

My mother sat up and said to him, "Why did you hit the child? She's done nothing wrong."

He crossed the room to my mother and slapped her across the face. "Here's one for you too," he said. My father turned, the sound of his shoes echoing down the hall as he stomped out of the house. He slammed the door behind him.

I was stunned, riveted by the drama, full of guilt that this new quarrel between my parents was all my fault. If I were not so greedy to wear the new snowsuit, none of this would have happened. I blamed myself for creating the drama that led to my father striking my mother. My guilt was too heavy to carry on my own.

My mother was crying, holding a worn handkerchief to her eyes. I felt sad and wanted to comfort her. *Please,* I wanted to say to her. *Don't cry Ma. I didn't mean for Poppa to hit you. I just wanted to wear the new snowsuit.* I wanted her to forgive me. I climbed onto the couch to be close to her. I lay next to my mother and put my arms around her. She pushed me. "Get away from me," she said. "Just get away."

5. THE FURNACE ROOM

Every winter we were freezing in that apartment in the Bronx. A chilly draft whipped through our apartment from under the front door, and an icy wind rattled the windows. Even with a couple of sweaters on, I still felt cold. We'd look for warmth anywhere we could find it.

When we were cold and needed heat, my mother would take a large wooden spoon from the kitchen drawer and bang on the radiator, a gray metal fixture that sat in the corner of the living room. Soon we would hear other neighbors in the building thumping and striking their radiators in solidarity. All of us with our nonverbal but loud demands were stating that we wanted heat right now, goddammit.

If no heat came from the radiator, we all knew the furnace in the basement was not filled with coal and fired up. At that point someone had to go downstairs to complain to the Super. I was that someone in the family. I had to ask him to please put on some heat, but at six years old, I didn't want to ask the super for anything.

Mr. O'Malley was a big man with a large belly. He'd hang out on the stoop of the tenement smoking cigarettes.

The shirts he wore barely covered his stomach and were dirty with food stains. His face was puffy and unshaven. His body smelled like he rarely took a bath. O'Malley looked angry all the time and grumbled to himself. Everyone in the building avoided him. No one liked being around him. He scared me.

I didn't want to go down to the dark basement alone. I knew what would happen next. My mother took my arm. "Go tell the Super to give us some heat," she said. I didn't want to leave the apartment. The furnace room and the Super frightened me, but I was more afraid to disobey my mother.

I wished for some powerful person to stand up and protect me from my mother. He'd lift up his giant hand and put it in front of her face. "Maria, are you insane?" my protector would say. "What are you doing? Why are you sending your six-year-old child down to the furnace room alone? Are you crazy? If you must send the child to get the Super to put heat in your apartment, then you must go with her. Or send someone else, not your child."

She'd probably reply something like, "What's wrong with sending the child downstairs? She's got nothing better to do. Besides, can't you see I'm busy here with the relatives?" My mother would never understand or see fear in my face. She would be angered by his interference. She just wouldn't get it.

———

Occasionally my parents entertained, usually for one of the Greek holidays. I looked around the room. Familiar people sat at the large table full of Greek food my mother had prepared. Mom would be smiling, in a good mood. My father would be in a corner with a glass of ouzo in one hand, a cigarette in the other, holding court.

"Isn't it a bit chilly in here?" one of the women would say. Everyone continued their chatter. If I felt any cold, I ignored it. No need to do anything. Eventually one of the guests would rub her arms and put on a sweater. I just liked being with the company. And I liked all the food at the table. No, I didn't want to leave the apartment and go down to that scary basement. I dreaded what would happen next.

My mother took my hand and said, "Go down and tell that Super we're freezing up here. We need some heat. You go and tell him that."

I didn't want to leave the apartment. She pushed me out the door and into the dark hallway. "Go," she said. I turned and walked away. Frightened, I expected a villain hiding in the shadows to jump out and attack me. I crept down the five flights of stairs with my heart pounding.

When I got to the lobby, I proceeded down ten more stairs to the Super's place. He lived alone in a small apartment next to the furnace room in the basement. When he wasn't mopping floors in the building, he was on the stoop drinking beer. I could always smell it on him, beer and cigarette smoke. I reached his apartment and knocked on his wooden door. I hoped he wouldn't be home. I hoped he wouldn't answer. His door opened a crack.

"Who's there?" he asked.

"It's me," I said with a shaky voice. "From apartment fifteen."

He opened the door wider and looked down at me like a giant monster. He had body odor and smelled of beer.

"What do you want?" he asked, scratching his fat stomach. He yawned.

"Mr. O'Malley," I mumbled, looking down at my shoes, "My mother says we need some heat. We're upstairs in apartment fifteen."

"Okay, okay," he said. "Just a minute."

He took some keys from his pants pocket. Then he closed his apartment door. He put a key in the door lock next to his apartment (the furnace room), swung open the door, and turned on a light.

The gloomy cave-like room had stacks of black coal piled high at every corner. I followed him into the dark space. His big hand closed the door. Then he took a shovel from the wall and pushed the blade into the stack. He heaved the black chunks of coal into the black hole of the open furnace. Matches appeared from his pocket. He struck one to start the fire and tossed the burning match into the furnace. The coals turned a bright red color.

I could feel the heat from across the room. I backed away to the door. He looked over at me and put down the shovel. His face was blank. *Oh*, I thought *This is it. He's going to kill me now. He's going to throw me in the furnace and no one will ever know what happened to me.* As if in a nightmare, I wanted to shout for help but I had no voice, and who'd hear me? The Super walked over to me, his shoes crunching on the chips of coal that scattered around the floor. I looked up at him. Great fear paralyzed me. *Please don't throw me in the furnace*, I prayed.

"Don't be afraid," he said. He stood over me and moved closer. "I won't hurt you."

His body odor surrounded me. The smell of beer hit me in the face. I couldn't move. Was he going to kill me now? I expected him to grab me by the neck, pick me up, and hurl me kicking and screaming into the hot furnace. Instead he stood there weaving, towering over me, his eyes glazed.

Then his fingers reached into the front of his pants and unzipped them. Was he reaching in there for a knife to kill me? Instead, he took out his penis, took my hand, and made me touch it. I'd never seen a penis before. At that moment, all I knew was how relieved I was that he wasn't going to throw me into the furnace and kill me. His penis felt like a soft stuffed animal. I squeezed it, and it reminded me of the texture of cookie dough. Just as quickly, he took my hand away, put his penis back in his pants, and zipped up his fly. Whew. What a great relief I felt. He hadn't murdered me.

Then he turned and went to the door. I followed him to leave. He opened the door to the street. Cold air hit my face. He closed the door to the furnace room, reached into his pocket, and pulled out a whole Hershey's chocolate bar, my favorite. He peeled open the paper and gave me a couple of squares of chocolate. I could see the letters H-E-R on the brown paper. I took the sweet piece and put it in my mouth. The chocolate felt warm, sweet, and gooey. It slipped down my throat as I turned away from him.

He went back into the furnace room and closed the door behind me. I climbed up the stairs, five flights to our apartment. As soon as I got to my apartment, I knew everything would be all right. I'd be safe. My mother and father would ask me what happened, why I was gone so long.

The living room felt warm with heat. Everyone was talking, talking, talking in their loud voices, laughing, laughing, laughing. All of their chatter sounded like stupid nonsense. I couldn't believe it. No one had noticed I had returned. No one realized I had survived a terrifying situation with the Super.

Feelings of sadness and anger at everyone in the room overwhelmed me. I especially felt rage toward my mother who had casually sent me down to the furnace room to face the creepy Super all by myself. My mother's attention was focused on talking with one of the relatives. I wanted to shake her. Didn't she realize I'd been gone almost an hour? Didn't she know what danger lurked in the furnace room? Didn't she even care what happened to me? Somehow I knew the answer to all those questions.

I looked around at everyone chatting about their own little concerns. No one seemed to have noticed I was gone. No one welcomed me home. I knew I could never tell anyone what had happened. No one would have believed me anyhow.

Days later I ran into the Super. He was in the hall-way sweeping the stairs. I looked at him. He kept his eyes on the broom. I remembered what happened in the furnace room—his smell, his penis, and the Hershey's chocolate bar. I cringed inside and raced by him to go to the street and play with my friends. I never went to the furnace room again.

6. THE JUMP ROPE

When my parents fought, my mother screamed Greek curses at my father.

"Where is the money?" she'd demand as he walked through the door. She'd be wiping one hand on her soiled apron, stirring a pot of bland lentil soup with the other. "I need to pay the rent." Her big worry was that we'd be evicted.

"Leave me alone," he'd spit back, putting his fist in her face, threatening to strike her if she said one more word. "How can I look for a job when you keep nagging at me every day?" She continued to hurl Greek swear words at him until he smacked her a good one across her face.

Everyone in our tenement building could hear their fights. "Why don't you guys shut the hell up?" someone would shout out their window.

"Get out! Get out!" my mother would yell, throwing obscenities at him.

He'd stomp out of the house, slamming the door behind him. I'd hide under the bed, listening. My stomach hurt from hearing their loud insults, which were like a knife blade thrown back and forth to pierce one another's heart.

I wondered why my mother was always angry with him. She must have done something to make my father leave. She was to blame. If she didn't yell so much, smiled more, and hugged him, then maybe he'd never leave. I saw my father as a happy, tender man. At least that's how he was with me. He was my Poppa and I loved him.

My mother suffered from depression; her moods were unpredictable. At any moment for no reason, she'd lash out at me, leaving me terrified. Unexpectedly, I'd get a slap. Without my father's presence, I became a target for her attacks.

Although my father was unemployed, he found temporary work as a house painter. He would come home whistling. He brought big bags of food: bananas, pears, oranges, a fresh fish, crusty bread, kasseri cheese, and black olives. My sisters and I jumped all over him with affection. The atmosphere in the house was calm for a little while.

With a few dollars in her pocket, my mother felt free to go shopping for produce in the local markets. I tagged along beside her and watched as she bargained to get the best price for green peppers, eggplants, and onions. She came home and cooked a lamb stew with garlic, onions, and tomatoes and spiced it with oregano. My sisters, brother and I would all eat elbow-to-elbow with gusto around the porcelain kitchen table. We sopped up the sauce with bread until our plates were squeaky clean. Those were good days.

When I was put to bed early, I lay wide-awake, waiting until I heard my father's footsteps as he entered the front door. *Yippee!* I thought. *Poppa is home.* I would get out of bed in my flannel pajamas, jump up and down with glee, and run into his embrace. His arms squeezed me tight. I inhaled the fragrance of sweet musk and his Old Spice aftershave.

He smelled of cigarettes, and his face was rough with beard stubble that scratched my young skin. I didn't care. My

Poppa was home, and that was all that mattered. "How is my little lollipop?" He tickled me under my arms, and I giggled with happiness.

He played games with me. We sat on the floor, and he took each of my toes, squeezed it, and sang, "This little piggy went to market, this little piggy stayed home." We laughed together. He was everything a little girl could want. He was my father.

Then one day when I was five years old, Poppa was gone. He wasn't home anymore. No one told me why he left. No one told me anything. As the youngest, they didn't think I'd understand. My father was everything to me. How could anyone explain his absence?

With the heavy silence in the house, I grew another level of sensitivity, an antenna to guess what might be going on. I knew better than to ask. If I did, all my sister would say is "Poppa left." It was like that in our home, a lot of unspoken explanations.

I missed him and blamed my mother for sending him away. If she only stopped screaming at him, dressed up a little, took a bath to relieve her body odor, maybe he would stay. The house was empty without him.

Several weeks passed. While playing hide-and-seek in the street one summer afternoon, I heard my father's voice from across the street.

"Sweetie pie," he called to me.

My heart jumped out of my chest. I could not believe it was him, my wonderful father. He looked so handsome in his pale blue, short-sleeved shirt and tan slacks. I didn't ask where he'd been. He was here now, and that's all that mattered.

"Poppa, Poppa," I cried. I ran to him, and he swooped me into his arms and kissed my face. We walked together hand in hand away from our apartment building and stopped at a corner candy store. This was a favorite place in the neighborhood to buy sodas, pretzels, and toys. He asked me to select a plaything to take with me. I saw a jump rope with twists of red, yellow, and green running through it.

"Oh, could I have it?" I asked and touched the rope.

"You can have anything you want," he said, smiling at me. I did not have many toys, and I was so happy to have my first jump rope. I held it tight in my hand, and I could hardly wait to go home and find someone to share it with. My father bought a chocolate soda, and we sipped it with two straws between us.

Then it was time to go. We walked back to the street where he found me. I held back tears when I hugged him goodbye. I wanted him to come home with me.

"I'll see you again soon," he said, holding my sad face in his hands.

I skipped down the street to our apartment building, looking for someone so I could show off my new toy.

Debbie, a girl who lived in the next apartment building, approached me. She was taller and older than me.

"Where did you get that?" she asked, pointing to my rope.

"My father gave it to me," I said.

"Can I try it?" she asked as she grabbed it from my hands. Then she laughed. "It's mine now. It's my rope." I didn't know what to do. I knew, with dread, I'd never see the jump rope again.

I was afraid of her. I felt as if her tight fist had thrust a punch to my stomach.

There was no father at my side to say, "Stop right there. Give that rope back to my daughter right now! It's not yours! I bought it, and it belongs to her." My father was gone, and there was no one to protect me. As angry as I was, I also felt shame. I was a coward, afraid to fight anyone. No one taught me how to defend myself. I wished for someone to stand up and fight for me. I knew Debbie could beat me up. I felt afraid.

Sobbing, I ran up the stairs to our tenement apartment. My sister, Dora, was coming down the stairs and caught me by the arm. I was crying so hard it was difficult to speak.

"What happened?" she asked. I blubbered that I had seen our father and he'd bought a jump rope for me, and now the neighborhood bully, Debbie, had stolen it.

"Don't worry," Dora said. "I'll get the rope back for you." She ran down the stairs, and I followed her to the apartment where the girl lived. She knocked on the door, and Debbie stood there with a smirk on her face, holding the rope in her hand.

"Give me the rope you took from my sister," Dora demanded, making a grab for it.

"No," the girl said defiantly. "It's mine now." She clutched it to her body.

Her mother, an obese woman with stringy red hair, heard the commotion and came to the door. "Well," she said. She wore a stained housecoat, her fat body bursting the dress at the seams, and held a can of beer in one hand and a lit cigarette in the other. I expected her to take the rope from her daughter and give it back to me, but she didn't do that.

"You two fight it out," she said, then yawned and turned away.

Dora and Debbie went into the street and began a tug of war over the rope. Each of them pulled hard on it. When the girl punched Dora in the face, my sister fell on the pavement, causing her nose to bleed. My sister got up and lunged, pulling the girl's hair. Debbie screamed, "Bitch!" Then my sister jerked on the rope until she wrenched it from her.

It was excruciating for me to stand there watching the two of them pulling and punching at each other, not knowing who would win. I stood there crying and feeling powerless. I was shaking with such fear my knees were knocking together. Again, I wished for my father or anyone's father to stop the fight and give me back my jump rope.

But my tears were also full of gratitude; at least my sister was fighting for me, for my jump rope, and she won. When I came home and went to my room that day, my mother was asleep in her bedroom, oblivious to the drama. She had enough of her own.

I put the jump rope in my drawer. At times, I would open the drawer and touch the rope. Then I put it back. I was afraid to take it out and ask someone to play with me. I could not risk losing it again.

7. THE PLAN

Whenever my older sister's birthday came around, her rich godparents would show up at our shabby apartment, their arms piled high with gifts. When my godparents, who were poor, visited, they usually came empty-handed. Dora's godparents didn't have children of their own, so they showered her with games, toys, and soft stuffed animals. As my sister hugged them with appreciation, I'd hide behind the living room door and weep with envy. Where were my gifts? Why didn't I get some too?

I remember Dora's godmother wearing furs and jeweled earrings. Her fragrant perfume filled the apartment. Dora's godfather, a tall, good-looking man with dark hair slicked back, would smile, pinch my sister's cheek, and pat her backside. Dora would giggle with delight and embrace them both.

On one of their visits, when I was seven, the godparents found me crying in the hallway, tears dripping down on my face.

"Why are you crying?" the godfather asked with a stupid smirk on his face. As if he didn't know. I covered my face with shame and turned to the wall. I didn't want him to see me full of tears and jealousy toward my sister. Yet my secret was discovered. I looked down at my scuffed brown shoes and bit my lip. I made up a story about something that happened at school that day. I lied and sensed they knew it too.

"Don't be such a silly little girl," Dora's godfather said with a laugh. "Don't be such a crybaby."

The godmother patted me on the head, and we all walked together to the dining room.

I found a chair and sat like a good little girl watching my sister open her boxes of presents. My sister's birthday cake would be in a pink box. Often the cake had a thick chocolate frosting I could eat with my fingers; forget the fork, I could hardly wait.

Then the following year, Dora's godparents came over but brought no gifts and no cake.

This puzzled me. We all went into the dining room and ate the dinner of roast chicken, buttered rice, and canned peas. I looked around to see if anyone was going to mention my sister's birthday.

"Happy Birthday," the godmother said to my sister and kissed her cheek. Then her godfather gave her a sly wink. After coffee, the godparents yawned and got up to leave.

"It's late," the godfather said. "The drive to Astoria is a long one."

My mother helped them put on their coats, and they left the house. My sister and I went into the dining room and brought the dishes into the kitchen to be washed. I still wondered why the godparents came without the usual parcels of birthday gifts. Neither my sister nor my mother mentioned it while we dried the dishes. What had happened? This wasn't a typical birthday for my sister; something didn't feel right.

"Let's get you to bed now," my mother said, shooing me into the bedroom.

I put on my pajamas. Dora's birthday felt like an unspoken mystery. And I sure didn't want to say anything about it. Why be reminded that my sister's birthday gifts were probably on their way?

"Go to sleep now," my mother urged as she covered me with a blanket. Soon I felt the darkness of sleep. Then I heard some voices that woke me up.

"Happy Birthday to you," the voices were singing. "Happy Birthday, dear Dora. Happy Birthday to you."

I crept out of bed and stood at the French door, looking through the flimsy transparent curtains into the living room. What I saw stunned me. Fancy plates sat on the dining room table. A large pink frosted cake stood in the center lit with candles. Was I dreaming? Dora's godparents were there and sat close to her applauding. My mother, her arms folded on the table, smiled her approval. I was transfixed. I could not take my eyes off the unbelievable scene before me.

My sister blew out the candles. She turned to a chair nearby. White boxes with red ribbons sat piled high, all waiting for Dora to open them. This was her birthday party. She had everything she wanted. Her wish had come true. Even though I wanted a piece of that cake, I knew with every fiber of my being I could not enter that room. They did not want me at the party.

Dora cut a slice of cake, placed the slab on a plate, and passed it to her godmother. She cut another piece and gave it to her godfather, and then one more for my mother. I could see the pink icing ooze down the sides of the cake, just waiting for a finger to take a glop of frosting to be devoured.

Their plan was clear. After I'd been put to bed, the godparents had returned to celebrate my sister's birthday without me. They had a scheme and never expected me to discover their deception; everyone at the table was part of the ploy.

My grief was immense, as if an elephant had placed his foot on my small body and crushed it to the ground. What had I done to be punished in this way?

Did they think I would not awaken, hear their singing, their laughter and celebration? How could they be so foolish to think I would not discover the truth? Were they so focused on pleasing my sister and excluding me that they had no thought of my feelings? Or did they believe they were excluding by removing me from Dora's celebration and avoiding my feelings of jealousy? Not likely. They knew I was envious of Dora and believed they were doing the right thing for both of us.

What does a child say to another when they are angry and want to hurt them? "You can't come to my birthday party." That was this moment. That's what their actions said to me.

How cruel to think I would not discover the truth. The following day, looking around the room, would I not have discovered the leftover cake and opened boxes with their gifts? How could I not discover their lie?

8. CARMEN MIRANDA

As a kid in the 1940s, my favorite day of the week was Saturday. On that day, I got to go to the movies, my favorite place in the whole world. Every Saturday the local Victory Theater in my neighborhood showed some cartoons and two films. For a little while, I got to escape my mother's moods, which were like a wild roller coaster, up and down, too scary for this seven-year-old. At the movie theater I got to leave my mother behind me.

Tina, my eldest sister, worked as a cashier at the Victory Theater. She told me I could get in free on Saturdays. I'd go up to the window, stretch my legs on tippy-toes, and she'd hand me an admission ticket. Every week I walked into the dark theater and grabbed the first seat anywhere on the aisle. The smell of buttered popcorn tempted me from the counter in the back of the place. But my main focus lay in the front of the theater. Images appeared on the large screen, actors spoke, and exciting scenes materialized. I devoured comedies, romances, and adventures like a hungry animal.

I was eager to see and totally immerse myself in whatever was playing on the screen. I looked for comfort anywhere I could find it. There I sat, glued to the chair, until the very last minute when the time came for me to go home. I never wanted to leave.

One Saturday, *A Weekend in Havana* burst onto the screen in Technicolor. The movie starred Alice Faye, John Payne, and a Brazilian spitfire named Carmen Miranda. She jumped onto the screen dancing, eyes sparkling, with a bright red lipstick smile and her arms shaking two maracas—*chick-chicka boom, chick-chicka boom*. She was magical. I couldn't take my eyes off her glittering, pulsating body.

A giant fruit hat with pineapple, cherries, bananas, and every other kind of harvest sat on her head. Giant white platform shoes made her look taller than the big movie screen could contain. Her floor-length dress showed a smooth bare midriff. A slit down the middle of her colorful, red-sequined gown let her legs peek out of the dress, tantalizing all of us. Her body moved to the Latin rhythm. Everything about Carmen Miranda enchanted me.

Her curvaceous body swayed as she sang. *Boom-de-boom* the bongos played. Latin guitars strummed in the background.

Carmen sang, "How would you like to spend a weekend in Havana, ay yay yay?"

I would have gone to Havana, found some maracas, and wiggled my behind right after her. I would have followed her anywhere. I watched the movie twice and memorized all the songs she sang.

In our apartment that night we celebrated someone's name day. My aunts, uncles, and cousins were visiting from Astoria—wealthy relatives dressed in fancy outfits, drenched in perfume. The women all wore sparkling earrings. The men wore dark suits, ties, and shiny black shoes. They all knew my mother didn't venture far from our tenement apartment. Her fear of the outside world was familiar to everyone in the family.

"How are you doing?" they asked, taking my mother's hand.

They all knew the answer: "Not so good."

My mother had prepared traditional Greek food for the company: a green salad with feta and black olives, eggplant moussaka, and rosemary chicken with buttered rice. Afterwards we ate the dessert she made—*karithopeta*, a honey walnut cake with coffee. Those were happy times.

I had just seen the Carmen Miranda movie, and I was still in ecstasy. I sat on a chair at the table in the kitchen and told my mother how much I liked Carmen while she prepared the food.

"Want to see how Carmen Miranda danced, Ma?"

I got up from the chair and jumped around the kitchen. I shook my arms, moved my hips and bottom. "Chicka, chicka boom," I sang.

"Hee-hee," my mother giggled.

"How did you learn all those words?" she asked, wiping her hands on her soiled apron. She pinched my cheek. I laughed and twirled around the room. I'd do anything to make her happy. I loved her then.

Later that evening, the company sat there in the living room, fidgeting in their seats. The men crossed and uncrossed their legs. They all looked bored. They had gorged themselves with food my mother made, and now they held their coffee cups on their laps, taking a sip now and then. Idle conversation between the women came up about their children, a husband's new job, letters received from the relatives back in the old country village, with a lot of dull silence in between. Someone yawned.

I sat still on the sofa between two cousins and felt my mother's dark mood enter the room like a sinister interloper, her private world crowding out any freshness. My mother stood up, smoothing the crinkles in her dress. She came over to me and took my arm.

"Come on and sing the Havana song for us," she said, pushing me to the center of the room. "You know, the way you sang it for me in the kitchen before."

What? I couldn't believe my ears. My mother wanted me to entertain the relatives? The company stopped their idle chatter and watched me curiously, all of them in a circle around me.

"The child can sing?" a rich aunt asked.

"Yes," replied my mother. "Just watch her." She turned to me and pointed to the center of the room. "Do Carmen," she ordered.

Oh no. All of a sudden I felt shy. I held myself back. My knees quivered. I wanted to run and hide. She nudged and patted my behind towards the center of the room. "Come on," she pressed. "Do Carmen. Do her."

What should I do now? I had to think fast. "Wait a minute," I said. I ran to the bathroom and grabbed a towel and put it around my head like a turban. I took another one and wrapped it around my bottom. I searched and could find no lipstick to wear, but I knew I could still dazzle them with my Carmen Miranda smile. No time to think of someone making fun of me.

I flew back into the living room in one beat. I sang my little heart out and shimmied my small behind just like Carmen Miranda. Her spirit flowed through me.

"How would you like to spend a weekend in Havana, ay yay yay?" I sang. My small body jiggled and wiggled. I danced and swayed around the room, rolling my eyes just the way Carmen Miranda did in the movie. I was hilarious. Everyone in the room laughed and clapped. They were amused. Even my mother smiled her approval.

"Where did she learn all that?" one of the relatives asked, clearly pleased with my recital. "She is just adorable."

"Isn't this little one something?" my mother said and placed her arm around my shoulder. I took a breath. My song was over. I looked at everybody. Carmen's passion had delivered me from the usual boring evening with relatives. She had lifted my mother's depression into laughter. For a precious little moment, she had delivered me into my mother's arms. For once, I felt loved.

9. WHEN MY MOTHER COOKED

"Go get my slippers," my mother mumbled to me from her bed. It was early afternoon.

She lay there, eyes closed, with bedclothes up to her neck.

I scurried on all fours under her bed to get them. The dust was thick like cotton balls, but I reached around and found them. There they were, two worn out slippers. *Goody*, I thought. *Mom is getting out of bed.* I placed the slippers by the bed, looked up at her lying there immobile. "Ma, here's your slippers," I said. But she still did not move.

Most days she lay there curled up in her old blanket, eyes closed, insulated from the world outside her room.

I relished the times when my mother raised herself from the pain of my father's desertion to get out of her unhappy bed. But most of the time there was an endless gloom over the house.

Nothing my older siblings or I could do would get my mother to budge. "Come on, Ma," we'd all say. "Get up." Not a stir. She rarely moved from her bed. The cocoon of her room protected her from dealing with her life.

Many times, I waited outside her bedroom door and listened. All I heard were my mother's moans and wails: "Achhh, achhh!" she'd cry. Her misery filled the whole apartment, permeating all the cracks and crevices within the walls.

When I was little, I loved my mother a lot. I would sit on her lap and kiss her face. When she wept, I'd hug her around her neck. "Don't cry, Ma," I would say. Now that I was older, I didn't sit in her lap anymore, but I still felt helpless and wished I could do something to make her feel better.

"What can I do Ma?" I begged. Usually she told me to fix her a cup of chamomile tea or go to the medicine cabinet and get some smelly goop to rub on her arms and legs. But mostly she told me to ask God for help.

"Pray," she'd say, pointing her finger at the ceiling. "Pray to God for my health."

I didn't know how to pray. An altar sat in the corner of her room with icons of Christ on the cross, Mary, and the baby Jesus. I wasn't sure I could pray the way she did, raising her hands in the air, repeating, *"Kyrie eleison"* (Lord save us). But I went to the altar anyhow and put my hands together. On my knees I whispered to God. I hoped He would hear me. *Please, God, please, God,* I pleaded. *Make my mom be okay.* I wanted Him to give me a miracle, to make her well again.

If my mother could only recover enough to get up and cook something, anything, I knew everything would be fine. That was the best prayer I could offer.

At dinnertime, my sisters and brother would scrounge around in the kitchen. We'd all look in the icebox and pantry to put something on the table. One of us would open a can of pork and beans and boil some rice to go with it.

My mother flip-flopped to the bathroom, opened the faucet, splashed some water on her face, moved on to her genital area, wiped down there and under her armpits with a cloth; so much for bathing. She got out of her crumpled, smelly bedclothes and put on cleaner ones. My mother never was one to fuss over her hygiene or her looks. She was a plain, simple peasant woman, short and chubby, with gray stringy hair down to her shoulders. My mother didn't even look at herself in the mirror. After my dad left us, my mother didn't care about her looks or about being a mother to her children. She had given up.

Eventually she waddled into the kitchen. Her soiled apron hung on a hook next to the sink. She reached for it with her small pudgy hands, put it over her head, and tied the strings behind her back—all this without conversation. I sat in joyful anticipation, elbows on the table, watching her every movement.

Nothing I'd ever tasted compared with a special dessert she made, her Greek New Year cookies. We called them *finikia* or *melomacarona*, honey cookies. To me, they were heaven in my mouth. These were sweet cookies covered with honey and nuts. Each bite melted from my lips straight down to my belly. In anticipation of tasting these scrumptious morsels, I waited for her command.

On New Year's Day, my mother would bake some of these cookies for the relatives in case they dropped by. Any leftovers were for us. She pointed to the cupboard.

"Go get me the big bowl," my mother said.

I got a chair, climbed up to the shelves in the pantry cupboards to reach for a thick bowl, and handed it down to her. She was particular about her dishes at these times. The bowl was a container my mother used just for baking, nothing else.

I never saw my mother use a cookbook or stir ingredients with a wooden spoon. She had a sixth sense about how to gauge the amount of flour, oil, and sugar without a measuring cup. She would just put it all together. Her fingers were short and thick; *squoosh, squoosh,* they mushed the batter together. Once she started cooking, my mother would sing *rebetika* songs. Those Greek blues were usually about a woman being dumped by her lover. I could tell my mother felt better when she started out humming a tune.

"You left me," she sang. "I who adored you. And now I can't go on,"—some sorrowful song like that. "And still I yearn for your embrace." I knew the song had to do with sad love. It had to do with my father leaving us. No one ever said so, but we all believed our parents would be together again someday. My mother never admitted it, but I could tell she missed him. I know I did. But in that moment, my mother was up and cooking, and it made my heart happy. In that moment I loved her. It didn't matter whether she loved me back.

I looked forward to the best part now that she had finished mixing the ingredients. She took her pinky finger, dipped it into the batter, raised it with a glop, and offered it to me for a taste. I gobbled it off her finger.

Greek cookies were shaped differently. They were not round and flat like American ones. My mother made them into the shape and size of a boiled egg. We had an old porcelain stove that my mother had to light with a match. She would reach down to the bottom where the pilot light was, strike a match, and light the oven. To help, I'd get out the banged-up aluminum cookie sheet from the side of the oven. My mother rolled the dough in her hands, placed the rows of *finikia* on the baking sheet one by one, and put them in the oven.

Then my mother wiped her hands on her apron. She took it off, hung it up on the hook, and went into the living room to knit. I stayed in the kitchen, sitting on my chair in anticipation.

I crept over and opened the oven door. Within five minutes I expected the *finikia* to be done. The sweet smells from the oven drove me crazy. I couldn't wait to taste one, but time dragged as I waited for the cookies to be baked.

"Get away from the oven," my mother called. "I'll know when they're done."

Sometimes my mother forgot to time them. She'd lose track of when she put them in the oven. That's when a batch of cookies would come out dark brown around the edges, a little burnt. Those were the ones she gave me. I didn't care. They crumbled in my mouth, a delicious blend of honey and sugar. I devoured every one of them and licked my fingers. As if any amount of food, even these special cookies, could fill the vast emptiness inside of me.

Melomacarona or Finikia

3 cups flour
1 cup semolina
2 cups olive oil
1 cup honey
½ cup powdered sugar
2 small glasses brandy
Juice from one orange
1 teaspoon grated orange rind
½ teaspoon cinnamon
½ teaspoon cloves
2 teaspoons baking powder

For the syrup:
1 cup honey
1 cup sugar
2 cups water
2 cups chopped walnuts

Work flour and semolina with oil until creamy. Add sugar, lukewarm honey, and remaining ingredients. Mix well for 15–20 minutes. Add a little more brandy if dough is too stiff, or add a little semolina if dough is too soft.

Roll with hands into size of an egg, flattening a little on one side.

Place on baking pan, and make a design crosswise with a fork.

Bake in moderate oven for 20–22 minutes.

Meanwhile, boil the syrup ingredients and as soon as the cookies are ready, dip each one carefully into the hot syrup for 2–3 seconds. Drain and arrange on a platter. Pour remaining syrup over cookies on platter. Sprinkle with chopped walnuts.

———

Years later, as an adult, when I'd think about making a batch of those cookies, I'd have to work up to it. I couldn't make them for just any reason. It would have to be a very special occasion, like a celebration or a New Year's Day party. I'd have to plan it carefully. I'd picture my mother standing at that chipped porcelain kitchen table, her thick fingers blending all the ingredients in that big bowl.

Come on, Ma, I'd think. *Help me make them like you did. Teach me.* I'd carefully put all the ingredients on the table. Then I'd put on one of those old bluesy *rebetika* records. I'd pour a glass of white, take a sip. I'd raise my glass to her and say, "Here's to you, Ma."

10. TWO SISTERS
AND A BROTHER

All I remember after my father left was that something felt sad in the house. Now it was just us siblings in the house with our depressed mother. With my father's absence, I looked to my sisters and brother to fill the empty space. To me they were perfect in every way. Tina was ten years older than me, Billy was next to the oldest, and Dora the middle one. I idolized them.

After my father took off to live with his latest girlfriend, my brother was forced to get a job after school to help pay the rent—yet another one of us who lost out on a childhood. One of his school friends' father had a construction company, knew our dire circumstances, and gave my brother a job painting and fixing up apartments in Manhattan. After my brother came home from school, he'd hurry and change clothes. At age fifteen his biggest fear was that someone would learn his age and he'd be fired. He learned every aspect of fixing houses—like painting, plumbing, and fixing electrical problems. He was our family handyman. Sadly there were some things in our home that were beyond repair.

I don't think my brother ever forgave my father for the heavy responsibility he placed on his young shoulders.

When World War II broke out, Billy joined the Navy. He enlisted in the part of the Navy that would bring home the most money. The submarines. After he left, my mother would sit on the stoop and cry, her eyes searching the street. She wanted her son to come home. We all worshipped my brother. He was a tall young man with thick brown hair and sparkling, deep-blue eyes. When he came home on leave, he looked great in his crisp white Navy uniform. His bell-bottom pants fit his backside just right. I simply thought he was the greatest, most handsome brother in the whole world. We all did.

As the youngest, I yearned for my siblings' approval, their nod of acceptance. I'd jump up and down around them like a puppy dog trying to get their attention. I looked at all of them with yearning eyes, eager for some crumb of recognition. But focus in the family was on my mother, not me. Like blind men, each holding a different part of the elephant trying to describe it, each of us had our own unique experience of her.

My brother was devoted to my mother. The Greeks say *a monaho yio*—the only male in the family is special. She offered him elevated status in every way. Billy got the best cuts of meat at the table. My mother fed him first. He had first choice of whatever he desired and as much food as he liked. Where my mother questioned my every move, he had free reign in coming and going in the house. We all took turns ironing his shirts, lighting his Camel cigarettes, and making sure he always had clean underwear. My brother took over my father's throne and became our king. We all bowed down to him.

After he got back from the Navy, my brother looked around and found a girlfriend in the neighborhood. Easy for him. The guy was gorgeous. My mother was suspicious and very possessive of him, never wanting him out of her sight. She ordered me to follow him, go to his girlfriend's house, and tell him he had to come home. Groan. I didn't want to play detective to my brother's activities. My mother's resentment of my brother's interest in women caused them to battle. It was the only time I remember him crying.

"What must I do?" he asked my mother repeatedly. "What must I do to please you?" We all wanted an answer to that question.

All of us carried heavy responsibilities, too weighty for our years. At one of the family reunions, my sister Tina told me her story. When she was eight years old, she said my mother sent her on a complicated errand that required her to take the train, purchase some item, and return home. When Tina returned home, my mother interrogated her, and then beat her because the merchant had cheated her out of a few pennies. When I asked Tina how she felt being sent on a complex mission at such an early age, and getting a beating on top of it, she replied, "Well, that's what all Greek mothers did. It was normal for a mother to beat a child so it would obey you." I disagreed and said that what my mother did to her and all of us had a name. It was called child abuse. She had no response.

My middle sister, Dora, had a knack of getting around my mother, usually with humor. "Come on, Ma," she'd say and hug her. "Lighten up, will you? You're driving us all nuts." Then she would head for the door. "Okay," she'd say blithely. "I'll see you later." And she'd dance out of the house. She knew how to *kalo piasi*—to sweet-talk—my mother. I never learned to do that.

I was jealous of Dora. She had rich godparents who indulged her, bought her expensive things, and took her places. My godmother was poor and schizophrenic—another depressed, unhappy Greek woman with an alcoholic husband who fooled around with other women.

I wished I had my sister's spunk, her "I-don't-give-a-shit" attitude. My ineffective way of getting out the door was to find a good excuse to leave the house; it never worked.

"The answer is no," my mother would say. "I need you here with me. You can't leave." Those countless futile pleas left me with feelings of rage and hatred for her along with a ton of Greek guilt for daring to have them. We were deadlocked in a head-to-head battle, my mother always the victor.

We all understood that my mother's depression meant she was unable to parent. She was afraid to be left alone. Although I was the youngest in the family, we knew my mother was the biggest baby in the house. Someone had to be there with her at all times. From an early age, that role was assigned to me.

My sisters were as different as night and day. Tina was tall, slender, and dark-haired with warm brown eyes. Her face was like the Mona Lisa, cool and serene-looking. Elegant, Tina wore dark tailored suits when she went out. She was the smart one in the family, always reading, studying, and writing in her notebook for her courses in Nursing. She wore White Shoulders cologne. It was heaven just to be near her, and even better if she let me hug her.

"Let go of me," she'd say. "You're choking me." It was true; I held on tight whenever she had to leave the house. I loved her and never wanted her to go. She bought record albums of Chopin, Mozart, and Bach. My love of classical music, opera and ballet all came from her. I admired and looked up to her in every way. She was a great lady. Our family Diva.

During the day Tina went to school, and at night she worked at the post office. Afterward she'd come home and do her homework. One morning I went into the kitchen for breakfast and saw her asleep, her face on the kitchen table with books and papers strewn all over. My respect and love for her was immense.

In contrast, Dora was the spitfire. She was the petite one who wore her hair short in what they called a pixie cut. Her clothing clung to her body like it had been sewn on. Everything she wore looked sexy. Her dress was usually something black and slinky with a slit up the side to her thigh. Her shoes were platform high and black suede. She lit up every room she entered. I'd follow Dora around the house as she dressed up before her date in Harlem with some Puerto Rican guy she'd met at the Palladium dance hall. Dora would search in her closet, take out a few dresses, and put them up against her body to see how each one felt. "How do I look?" she'd ask. Everything Dora wore looked great.

In the bathroom sitting on the toilet seat, I'd watch her carefully put on makeup—first she would select her eye shadow, a pale blue, then the lipstick, a bright vermillion she would carefully spread over her lips, pressing them together before blotting them with bathroom tissue. As a final touch, she would put a dab of Shalimar behind her ears and on her wrists.

I'd be gaga, asking her if her date was cute, what he looked like. "How tall is he?"

"Oh, about six feet," she'd say. "All muscle."

"What color are his eyes?" I'd ask.

"Deep brown," she'd say, smiling at a memory of their last time together.

"How did you meet him?" I'd ask.

She told me she met him at the Palladium one night, what a great dancer he was, and how he held her close, moving her this way and that as they danced the mambo and a slow bolero together belly-to-belly. She laughed and said, "I think

I felt his hard-on when we danced the last time. He wants to go to bed with me, but I don't want to get pregnant."

Those teenage hormones were wild inside me. I was boy crazy. Everything my sister said was of great importance to me. I wanted boyfriends like hers.

I'd be mesmerized as she gave me all the details of his looks, how he lit a cigarette and gave her a puff from it. Her life was like some of the movies I saw on Saturday mornings—romantic, exciting, and dangerous.

I worried about her going to Harlem at night because it was not a safe place. I'd hear from friends about fights at some dance with some jealous guy cutting or stabbing another guy. It was always something stupid. Someone looked at his girlfriend, or a bad drug deal went down. Once, my sister told me she saw a guy fall off the roof of a Harlem tenement building. Crazy scary shit like that.

I hung on Dora's stories—the drama, the excitement, and the danger in all of them. I was afraid for her because she liked living on the edge. Some of her boyfriends were into some shady dealings: drugs, pimping, pushing hot merchandise. None of the guys she went out with had jobs, only hustles, like dealing drugs. One of her Harlem girlfriends was a shoplifter. She'd take clothing from the finer department stores in Manhattan, like Lord and Taylor and Saks Fifth Avenue. Dora bought some of those elegant dresses from her for less than half of what they would have cost at the store. A part of me trembled at the thought that my sister might end up in jail someday as an accomplice to her friend's crime.

When my sisters were away, I would sneak a peek into Tina's and Dora's clothes closets. When I needed a sexy black dress to attend some party or dance, I looked for an outfit that made me look older, more sophisticated than my fifteen years. I wanted to be just like my sisters and have boys notice me.

The trick for me was to get the dress, wear it, and then get it back to their closet before they found me out. Unfortunately, it didn't always work out that way.

"Did you wear my dress, you brat?" I'd hear my sister yell in the morning. "There is a stain on it, and I'm going to kill you if you ever wear it again." I would panic and swear I hadn't touched the dress. But the dumb expression on my face showed I lied. I always got caught. Still, whenever the occasion came up again that I had a special date or a dance where I wanted to impress a new boyfriend, I'd take another risk and roam into that dangerous territory—my sisters' closets—to see what outfit I could find that would knock the boy's eyes out and make him fall madly in love with me.

Only for an evening, I thought. *Just one night out, that's all.* Once again I browsed their closets and searched for a slinky black dress. When I found the absolutely perfect one that made me look older and attractive, I felt the risk of getting caught was worth it. For just a few hours wearing one of those great sexy dresses made me feel like a million bucks.

11. THE MATCHMAKER

The dark gray, six-story building where we lived, 752 Trinity Avenue in the Bronx, was in a poor neighborhood. In the cold winters, we huddled together around the radiator in the apartment to keep warm. In the summertime, we went up on the tarred roof to try to cool off. This was also where we hung the laundry out to dry. It was fun to look over the ledge at the view from the top of our building, to see the lights from other buildings and peer into other apartments. I was curious to see what normal families looked like.

As the youngest, after everyone else scattered, I got stuck caretaking my mother. I would bring her tea in bed, play Greek music on our phonograph to cheer her up, massage her arms and legs with some god-awful smelly cream.

"Take care of Momma," my sisters would say as they left the house. The message was clear that it was my job to raise my mother's spirits and do anything she asked to get her the hell out of bed. I failed miserably at my role. Nothing I did managed to dispel my mother's misery and bitterness. She pushed the world and everyone in it far away from her.

While she rested, I'd go to the window and watch my friends playing games, jumping rope, tossing a ball, and I wished I could be with them. Instead I felt chained to my mother's bed, at her beck and call for anything she might need. Without a word spoken, I felt responsible for my mother's well being, but none of my efforts seemed to work.

As much as I blamed my mother for my father's departure, I also felt sorry for her, pitied her for having been dealt a bad hand loaded with a lot of misery. I wished there were something I could do to ease her sorrow. I wanted to lift her spirits, make her laugh, and give her hope for the future. Deep inside, I loved her. I had a childlike optimism that I could help restore her health, get her on her feet, out of her sickbed, and well again. I had a naive belief that if I catered to her needs my mother would get up and leave our dark apartment, go downstairs, sit on the stoop of our tenement, and visit with neighbors. Maybe she'd bring some life into our dismal hovel. She'd go to the kitchen and cook something for me to eat. She'd give me a hug.

One day something in the daily newspaper caught my eye. It was an ad that read: "Clara Lane, Jewish Matchmaker." It continued, "If you are lonely and would like to meet a good, eligible man, call me. I can help introduce you to someone who can be the beginning of a new life for you. Please don't wait. Call or write me now."

Her photo next to the advertisement showed a smiling woman in her sixties, her gray hair in a bun on top of her head. She looked like a kind, wise lady with a sympathetic face. With a feeling of desperation and foolish optimism, eager to do something to help my mother who I knew needed a man, I magically felt Clara Lane and I could find one for her.

Just looking at my mother buried in her bed under a ton of despair, I knew she wanted someone to care for and love her. We had no phone, so I wrote Clara Lane. I pretended to be my mother, lonely and unhappy, searching for the right man to rescue me from a life without hope or happiness. "I would like to meet a nice man," I scribbled. That should cover it. I hoped the matchmaker couldn't tell a young school girl who was not Jewish had written to her. Ironically, my mother was illiterate and unable to even sign her own name!

After writing my note to Clara Lane, I put it in a stamped envelope and mailed it. Then I forgot all about it. Asking this woman for help was more like a prayer, begging someone out there in the universe to come and rescue all of us, not just my mother. A few weeks later, I was excited to receive a reply from Clara Lane in her own handwriting. She said she had several eligible men she would like me to meet.

Uh-oh. Now what should I do? I was delighted Clara Lane had replied to my request. But these were eligible Jewish men she wanted to introduce my Greek mother to. I searched but never did see an ad in any newspaper for a Greek matchmaking service. These arrangements were usually made between close friends and relatives. Besides all that, I had to face reality: my mother was still married to my absent father. I feared getting caught by one of my sisters reading Clara Lane's letters and would be punished for lying. In time, the whole idea of finding a match for my mother felt like a big mistake.

We all would have liked my father to return home, a changed man. He'd get a regular paying job, pay the bills, stop drinking, gambling, and running around with other women, and become a responsible father and loving husband—some kind of miracle. Even at that young impressionable age, I knew that could never be.

Idealistically I wanted my father back, not a new stranger to court my mother. But I was desperately willing to accept any man Clara Lane sent us who would courageously walk through our door and help change our lonely lives.

Some of the movies I saw on Saturday showed couples who initially hated each other's guts, but magically in the film they transformed their relationship. With music, song, and moonlight, all in Technicolor, the couple ended up madly in love with each other. I hoped for some dream like that for my parents. What a great fantasy life I led.

On occasion, Tina was given free theater tickets by a teacher. I still remember the delight we all felt about getting my mother to reluctantly agree to American entertainment. She gave her approval for all of us to see the play *Babes in Toyland*, my very first musical.

What a feat it was to get my mother out of bed, to perform her "douche" (washing under her armpits, then down to her crotch.) She covered herself to make sure none of us were watching her. From her closet my mother selected one of her drab, colorless, synthetic, ankle-length dresses, pulled on thick, dirt-colored beige stockings which she rolled up to her knee in a knot to keep them up, and finally put on laced-up black shoes. She looked more like she was going to a funeral than a play.

The hardest part for us was getting my mother to put on lipstick. "No, no," she'd say, pushing us away. "Only *putanas* (whores and loose women) paint their lips. No, I won't wear it." "Don't move, Ma," we would insist, with both of my sisters holding my mother's arms to her side while I, the designated lipstick applicator, tried to hold her tight face still and attempted to put some color on her stiff mouth.

"Come on, Ma," I'd coax. "Just let me put a little bit of lipstick on you." It was like a slapstick comedy. My mother protesting, clenching her mouth tight, pushing us away, with the daughters coercing her, as though she were a child being forced to eat her spinach.

All of us sisters secretly hoped that if we dressed my mother up a little, put some makeup, lipstick, and color on her face, perhaps some nice man might find her attractive enough to see something about her that was worthwhile, someone worth loving. Then maybe, just maybe, we could all find some small amount of love of our own.

We were late for the performance; the usher rushed us to our seats. My mother kept jabbing me with her elbow asking me to explain what the play was about. "What are they saying?" she asked, poking me in the ribs, as people nearby gave us dirty looks and shushed us to be quiet. How did I get stuck being my mother's translator? I just wanted to watch the musical, see the dancers in colorful costumes, and hear the music without her bugging me. Because the play was not in Greek and she had a limited knowledge of English, my mother was bored with it all. She mumbled, "Eh, eh," sucking on her teeth, dismissing the whole experience. She was unable to find enjoyment in anything unfamiliar. At times like that I wished for anyone else's mother but mine.

When we got home, we were all exhausted. To get my mother out of bed was hard. Getting her dressed, pushing her out of the house, walking five blocks to the station, and taking a train to make the performance had been a Herculean task.

Whenever another opportunity for an outing presented itself, we had to repeat the routine all over again, all of us hoping that this time it would be different, that my mother would find some enjoyment in seeing something new. Maybe she'd get dressed without our fussing over her looks and welcome an occasion to leave the dreary house. Her capacity for laughter and joy, unfortunately, was nonexistent.

Weeks had passed since I'd first contacted Clara Lane. I ignored her letters even though she continued to write and encourage me as if I were my mother. The matchmaker thought my letters came from a single Jewish woman. What an insane idea I thought sadly, that some nice stranger might come to our door and, without introduction, whisk my mother away from her unhappy life. It was my childlike desperate fantasy for that miracle.

Eventually Clara Lane stopped sending letters urging me to contact her to meet a special eligible man who she believed was just right for me. After a while, a long while, I guess we both gave up.

12. THE TREE

One Christmas Eve when I was ten, I was home alone with my mother in the living room of our Bronx apartment. My brother had enlisted in the Navy and was somewhere in the South Pacific. My two older sisters were away for the holidays with relatives, and as usual the responsibility for caring for my mother had fallen to me. It was freezing outside, and there was little heat in our tenement. The apartment was dark, save for a lone lamp in the living room where I sat by myself, waiting for something to happen.

Everything was silent except for a noise coming from the kitchen, where the refrigerator was groaning as if it were about to expire. My mother lay in bed with covers up to her chin, her body slathered with Vicks and Bengay. For most of my life, this is the way I've remembered her: not sick enough for a doctor, but not well enough to be on her feet. I fidgeted in my chair. Perhaps a knock on the door from a neighbor would break the deafening silence.

This is Christmas Eve, I said to myself, *and we don't even have a lousy Christmas tree.* I sighed loudly, hoping my mother would hear me and do something. Anything. She hadn't even tried to get up and cook or bake, anything to bring some holiday spirit, some small cheer, into the gloom of the apartment. After what felt like hours of dull despair, I couldn't stand it any longer. I went into the dark bedroom where my mother lay aching and moaning as usual, lamenting her bitter fate. For as long as I remembered, she'd complained to anyone willing to listen about the hard life she had bringing me up without the support of a husband. Once again that night, she spoke of the countless sacrifices she had made for me, how she'd almost died in childbirth with me, and how I should never forget it.

"Ma," I said, "It's Christmas Eve, you know? Aren't we going to even get a tree? Everyone else has one."

She quickly shot back, "A tree? What are you talking about? Can't you see how sick I am? If you weren't so selfish, you would run to the nearest church, fall on your knees, and pray to God to restore my health."

Now it was my turn to groan. I knew her lines by heart.

"And besides," she added, shaking her finger at me from her bed, "where am I going to find the money? Your father, that *koproskilo* (a rotten dog), left us penniless." And once again, I heard what a tyrant he was, how he had mistreated her, betrayed her with other women, drank, and gambled his money away. All men, she reminded me, were just like my father, no good and after only one thing. I would find that out for myself someday, just wait. She was a depressed woman, bereft of hope, another Greek tragedy.

I sat there until I felt the apartment and my mother's depression suffocating me. With my last ounce of hope, I pleaded with her once more. "Please, Ma, let me try to get a tree," I begged. "Can't you even give me a dollar for one?"

"No!" she shouted back. "Have you lost your mind? It's too cold and dark out. Besides, where can you buy a tree for a dollar?"

"We should have a tree," I repeated, feeling I was talking to an impenetrable wall.

The tree now seemed tremendously important, despite the obstacles my mother put in its way. I believed the tree would make a difference in my life. Perhaps it would not only cheer the dismal place up, but by some miracle, my mother might even venture away from her creaking bed and get into the holiday spirit. Once more I went back into her bedroom and stood at the foot of the bed, silently waiting. Without speaking, she took her purse from beneath the pillow and carefully gave me a crumpled dollar bill.

Before she could change her mind, I grabbed my jacket and, with the dollar tight in my fist, ran down the stairs, two at a time, to the street. It was so cold I could see my breath in the winter air. The streets were deserted. A thin crust of snow had turned to ice, and I walked carefully, so as not to slip and fall. Everything was quiet, except for the icy wind that stung my face like needles. I dug my hands deeper into my jacket pockets and fought the wind, head down.

I headed for Union Avenue. It was always fun to shop there on Saturdays with my mother because the clerks were generous with their samples of olives, cheese, and fruit. This time, all but one store was closed.

As one of the produce storeowners was about to shut his door, I asked him, "Mister, do you have any Christmas trees?" I hoped he might have a few hidden in the back of his store. "Do you know where I can get one?"

"No, little girl, don't you know there's a strike on?" he said as he closed out the till. "We got none this year." He turned away.

But I didn't want to give up and go home yet. I walked on to Prospect Avenue. Then I saw two enormous Irish policemen walking toward me. This felt promising. I stopped in front of them, feeling very small and scared.

"Officer," I began, but I could not say more as I choked up with tears and began to cry.

"What's the matter?" one asked.

Through my sobs, I told them of my search for a tree.

Once again I heard, "Don't you know there's a strike on, little girl? There are no trees."

I kept crying and shaking my head no. "I have to have one," I said desperately.

They exchanged looks, and between them each took one of my hands. We walked, checking with the few last store-owners who were closing up on Prospect Avenue. Somehow I felt hopeful as we walked up and down the streets. Late shoppers eyed me with suspicion. Their silent stares seemed to ask what crime might this little girl have committed to be walking between two officers of the law.

I began to shiver and my teeth chattered. I felt so cold that finally I gave up. What a silly idea that I could get a tree on Christmas Eve. My mother was right. I was crazy.

Through my shivering, I turned to one of the policemen and said, "Maybe I better go home now; it's getting late."

He nodded. Then, as we turned to walk back, a huge truck rounded the corner piled high with Christmas trees. One of the policemen whistled and hailed the truck. Tires screeched, and the truck came to a halt. The policeman ran over and talked to the driver for a moment, pointed to me, went to the back of the truck, and took down a tree. To this day, I'm still not sure what magic that policeman wove to get it for me.

The tree seemed huge to me. The policeman steadied the tree for me to hold it. I was stunned, in shock that the tree was actually standing in front of me. Even now, I can remember the smell of the pine and how the bark of the tree hurt my small fingers as I held onto it. I shoved the crumpled dollar in the policeman's hands, thanked them both, and ran home, half carrying and half dragging the tree behind me.

When I finally got home, steam was singing from the radiator, and the apartment was warmer than before. My mother was responsive enough to sit up in bed, mystified. Then she reminded me we only had a few tree ornaments and most of them were broken.

"That's okay," I said, and I searched deep into the closets until I found two dented cardboard boxes with old ornaments and used tinsel. I decorated my tree with care, and to me, it was the most beautiful Christmas tree in the world. I wish I could say my mother smiled when she saw the tree, or embraced me and praised me for my courage in venturing out alone in the cold night to find it. But hers was a small world of sorrow she could not escape. She never knew that the tree was a symbol of a deeper faith within me that helped me survive that Christmas Eve and my desolate life.

13. THE LAST TIME
FATHER LIVED WITH US

Our apartment was dark except for the single light bulb coming from the kitchen. My older sisters were engrossed in conversation with my brother. No one noticed my entrance or spoke to me. As I strained to hear what they were saying, I caught phrases here and there.

"We're going to have to find Poppa. Anyone remember where he lives these days and how we can reach him?" Their heads were close, as they spoke intently. "Someone has to get word to him to tell him Mom's in the hospital."

My father had been gone for several years; we never knew how to reach him because he lived with various women and kept his whereabouts secret. He didn't want us to know who his latest flame was, but now we needed to find him because my mother was sick in the hospital. No one knew what was wrong with her. She always blamed one of us for her many ailments.

"You," she'd say, pointing her finger at me. "I almost died giving birth to you."

As though by being born I had deliberately caused her pain. They continued to talk together. Some part of me began to jump up and down with happiness. My father was coming home? Was it possible? *At last, at last,* I thought. *My savior is coming back, and everything is going to be all right. Oh joy!*

After my father left, my mother was full of rage and bitterness, and I became the receptacle for the release of those feelings. I felt protected when my father lived with us. When he was gone, living with my mother was dangerous. Like a volcano, she would unpredictably erupt. I avoided her as much as possible. Now my mother was sick and in the hospital.

Things were never explained to me, such as the reason my mother was so ill as to need hospitalization. I always saw her in bed with covers up to her neck, full of despair and desolation. She rarely left her room.

Without asking anyone, I tried to figure it out on my own. What was wrong with mother this time? Why did we have to contact my father now? Was my mother dying? Doubtful. If my father went to the hospital, would my parents miraculously be reconciled? Unlikely. Things like that were never clarified. I knew no one would tell me the real reasons for my mother's illness or the purpose for my father's return. Like dark, heavy clouds, these mysterious questions hung around the house without answers.

Someone finally tracked my father down through one of his girlfriends. We'd managed to get by without him for so long. It baffled me why he was needed now.

But one night I opened the door to the apartment and I heard my father's voice. I could hardly contain my glee in seeing him again. There he sat at the kitchen table with a cigarette in his mouth. My siblings stood all around him waiting for him to speak while he casually held court, as though he'd never left. He opened his arms to me.

"I brought your mother home from the hospital," he said, taking a drag from his cigarette. "I'll be here for a while until she's feeling better." I hoped he'd never have to leave us again.

———

There was a public telephone in the hallway of our apartment. After he left us, from time to time my father unexpectedly called for me and my sisters to meet him at the local subway station. Just waiting at the bottom of the stairs was excruciating, the time dragging until he ran down the stairs and swooped me up in his loving arms. Even before he hugged me, I could smell his aftershave. He would take us all out to the movies, then for sandwiches at a local diner. Before he left us he'd slip a twenty-dollar bill in my pocket for my mother. I dreaded those moments when he hugged me goodbye.

"I'll call you soon," he would say, with a pat on my cheek, but it would be weeks before we heard from him again.

Now he was home. I came into the kitchen and there he was, all smiles to see me. He brought many things with him—boxes, crates, and luggage. I felt overwhelming love for him and was ecstatic that he was home. I completely adored him. His eyes sparkled as he pinched my cheek. "How's my lollipop?" he asked.

The big question was what the sleeping arrangements would be now that my father was back home. We all looked to my mother to make that decision. As we gathered around her bed, she looked small and frail with the covers pulled up to her chin. Despite her condition, we all knew and felt her power. No illness could diminish her control.

The medicinal smell of cold remedies permeated her bedroom like a toxic gas. Her gray hair was uncombed and matted around her head. Her eyes were half closed as she stared at us from her pillow. We all stood around my mother's bed, waiting. Slowly she croaked out the sleeping arrangements. She took her hand out from under the covers and pointed her finger first to my two sisters.

"You two will sleep in my bed with me," she said. To my brother she said, "You will sleep in the back room." Then she pointed at me. "Your father will sleep with you in your bed." I stood there frozen. What kind of Greek insanity was my mother talking?

I wanted my father to say firmly, "No, Maria. Listen to me. Stop this nonsense. The girls will sleep together in one bed, and you and I will be in our own bed as man and wife. Do you understand?"

Adolescent daughters do not sleep in the same bed with their fathers. That made no sense to me whatsoever. I wanted him to stand up to her, argue with her, but he said nothing. Was my father afraid of her too? I hoped for anyone to speak out and say something to stop her orders, but no one did. I remained silent, accepting her decision as I accepted her blows. As the good Greek daughter, I had been trained well to never question or disagree. Just obey. I loved my father dearly, but I did not want him in my bed.

In Greece as a youngster, it is an honor to sleep with a parent or grandparent who is the same sex as the child. It is the custom in that country to allow that, but we were not in Greece. We were in America, and in this situation something was terribly wrong. We all remained silent. Certainly as the youngest I had no voice to speak. Who would even listen? There was nothing I could do or say to make things right. I looked to my parents to do that.

I felt sad leaving my mother's room. I turned and went to the bathroom to change into my flannel pajamas and brushed my teeth. As I passed the living room, I saw my father sitting on a chair reading the evening newspaper. Then he took out some tobacco from a pouch and rolled a cigarette. A sense of relief swept over me that I would go to bed first. The bedroom was small with just enough room for the bed, a small closet, and a dresser.

After putting my books together for school the next day, I crawled into bed and found a spot closest to the wall. I was not tired at all. My mind and body were awake and alert to every sound in the house. My sisters were talking and preparing for bed, and I felt alone, excluded, wishing there were some small space they'd find for me in my mother's bed. I wanted to join them. I could hear the rustling of my father's newspaper in the living room. I heard my mother's moans, and hoped she might realize her mistake and change her mind, so that I could be allowed to squeeze into her bed with my sisters.

Finally, I dozed off into a light sleep. Later, when my father came to bed, I was keenly aware of his presence. In the dark, he silently changed into his pajamas, slowly wound the Big Ben clock, and then came to bed. It took a long time before I let go completely and drifted into a deeper slumber.

My father woke up early. It was dark outside when he left for work. This pattern was set for several weeks: I was asleep before he came to bed at night, and still sleeping when he got up and left for his job as a house painter.

One night, comfortable with the routine, I was in a deep sleep when my father came to bed. Something awakened me. Was it the smell of alcohol on his breath? I froze with terror as my father's hands began to slowly creep under my pajama top. He began to gently touch my right breast and nipple, then my left one. I felt as though a thousand watts of electricity had charged my chest. My body was screaming, *Stop it. Somebody help me.* I was paralyzed with fear. I wished I could disappear into the wall, but there was no place to hide. The incident went into the deepest part of my psyche where it needed a safe place to deal with it.

The routine varied, but each time my father came to bed, I froze with terror, unable to stop his hand from reaching under my pajamas to touch my breasts. I would pretend to be asleep, to be somewhere else, and feel nothing. Each morning I awakened, and from the night before, put the memory into a deep freeze. Even if I'd had the courage to speak out, there was no one I could tell. Who would believe me? Surely not my mother. More importantly, my father living with us was paramount to our existence. If he left, who would support us?

The church gave scholarships to families on welfare; I was given the gift to go to summer camp. When I returned, my sister met me halfway up the stairs and stopped me before I could hear the news from my mother. She whispered to me that my father had packed his things and left while I was away.

My physical being could not ignore the truth that this man, my adored father, by his act of touching my budding breasts, had methodically murdered my soul as deliberately as if he had walked into the kitchen, taken a butcher knife from the drawer, came back to my bedroom and stabbed me repeatedly in the heart. My king of kings destroyed my innocence and my love for him. I'd never be the same again.

14. DEPARTURES

After my father left for the last time, one by one we all waited for our turn to escape. My mother, always an anxious woman, became even more unhinged after my father left. She was a ticking time bomb ready to explode at any moment. None of us wanted to be around her.

Tina was the first one to leave. During her training to become a nurse in the late 1940s, she met someone at a psychiatric hospital in Long Island. Oscar was a survivor from a Polish concentration camp; He was a chief psychiatrist at the hospital in Long Island. They met on a blind date, and he fell head over heels in love with her. He was twenty years her senior, but that didn't stop him from his pursuit to marry her. He was smitten. My mother wanted to know all about him.

"Is he Greek?" she asked.

"No," my sister replied. "He's a doctor and a nice man."

"Does he have any money?" My mother was always worried about money.

"Yes," my sister replied. "He has a job in a hospital and has some money."

"But is he Greek?" my mother persisted. "Where does he come from? What is he?"

"He's Jewish," my sister replied. "He comes from Austria."
My mother slapped her face. "You can't marry him. He's not a Greek."

Silences were common in the apartment. There were lots of them filled with secrets I could only guess at. No one spoke to me about what was going on, but somehow I understood that my sister would marry the doctor from Austria.

She did the unspeakable and defied my mother. She went through with plans to marry the psychiatrist. She brought him over to the apartment to meet us one evening. She hoped my mother would be impressed. He had grayish hair, was not too tall and a bit paunchy. Dora and I sat on the couch, covering our mouths and giggling; both of us disapproved of the match. We had hoped for some good-looking guy to marry our big sister because we wanted her to choose someone whose good looks matched her beauty.

The day Tina was to marry, our house was silent and thick with tension. She looked exquisite in a light beige dress. Dora and I wanted to go to her wedding to celebrate because we loved her. Without asking, we knew we couldn't go. My mother would never allow it.

Dora and I sat in the kitchen and watched the scene unfold. The time had come for my sister to leave the apartment for her wedding. My mother, her face all scrunched up in a scowl, stood guard at the door with her arms folded. My sister in her beige wedding dress with flowers in her arms knelt before my mother.

"I'm leaving," Tina said. She took my mother's hand. "Please give me your blessing."

My mother pushed her away, turned, and opened the door. "Just get out," she said. "You'll get no blessing from me. Leave."

I wept with rage at my mother's cruelty. I wanted to leave the house with my sister Tina, to be a member of her wedding. "Take me with you," I wanted to say. "Don't leave me here." I loved my sister. My heart broke to see her begging for my mother's blessing.

No one told us this, but we found out that the real reason my mother wouldn't attend my sister's wedding was because my father would be there. Horrors! My mother couldn't accept that insult. How dare my sister invite him to her wedding when my mother had done all the hard work of raising her and the rest of the brood without any help from him? My mother could not put her bitter resentment aside even for one day to celebrate her daughter's wedding.

About a year later Tina got pregnant and had her first child, a girl. My mother warmed up and become a caring grandmother. All would be forgiven.

The next one to leave home was my brother Billy. Just out of the Navy and still wearing his uniform, he looked so handsome and rugged, like an ad for clothes in some men's magazine. His tall, wavy brown hair and easy smile attracted several young women at the local church. This drove my mother crazy with fear and jealousy. She didn't want him out of her sight.

"Follow him," she'd say to me. "Tell me where he goes and who he talks to."

I didn't want to do any of that. "Aw, Ma," I'd say, "I don't want to follow him. I want to be with my girlfriends."

"No," she'd say, pushing me out the door. "You follow your brother to the girl's house. Tell him he has to come home." My mother knew if he got involved with some girl and left home, she'd lose any money he gave her from his paycheck. Any control she felt she had over him would disappear.

When my brother opened his girlfriend's door, he stood there and gave me a stern look. "What are you doing here?" he asked. He knew the answer.

"Momma said you should come home," I said, looking down. What a dumb thing to say. I could see the girlfriend sitting on the sofa in the background, her mouth open in disbelief. If that didn't ruin any relationship, I don't know what would. Any woman would think my brother had an insane mother. In fact, he did.

My brother battled with my mother. They'd argue back and forth.

"Stop following me," he said. "I'm not a little boy anymore. Just stop it." My mother would attack.

"Can't you see these women just want your money?" What money? She couldn't believe some woman might just love my brother and not have ulterior motives.

No matter what he said about her intrusive behavior, she attacked my brother right back.

"I'm your mother. Show some respect," she'd say, with her fist in his face. "Who are these women? Are they Greek? Do they care about you? No. They just want to marry you and get your money—that's all." Money was all she thought about. Despite my mother's suspicious behavior and attempts to control my brother, one woman got through the fortress and won my brother's heart.

Christina was an attractive young lady. Billy met her at the local church and they fell in love. When they went out to a movie together, I was the chosen chaperone. I liked her. My mother objected, of course, and did everything she could to break them up. She'd holler and scream at my brother and try to find everything wrong with her. "She doesn't love you," she'd say. Nothing my mother schemed to sabotage their relationship worked. After a year they married.

I wept at his wedding. I adored my brother. The only male left in our home would be gone. Now there were only two of us left with my mother in our dungeon of an apartment—my middle sister and me.

I felt trapped. Something inside me knew I had to find a way to escape. Every cell of my being wanted to leave, but how? I was just a fourteen-year-old kid. I'd need some help. I'd need a plan to get out of prison and slam the door hard behind me.

15. THE STENO PAD

When I was sixteen, my mother's beatings increased. She'd come at me like a tiger, pouncing on me as soon as I walked in the door.

Whack, across the face. "Where were you?" *Whack*, on my arm. I'd try to defend myself. I'd say anything to get her away from me. I told her I was at the library. "Don't you lie to me, you rotten tramp." *Whack*, one on the head. "I'm going to get you for this." As though I'd committed the worst sin, the worst offense. Got caught again with a boyfriend. *Whack. Whack. Whack.*

When my mother was finished with me—meaning she had beaten and vented her wrath on me, pounded me, hit me, given it to me good—she'd scream some Greek curses at me and I'd run into the bedroom.

That's where the steno pad was. My sister was studying Pittman stenography in school and she'd bring home extra pads to scribble on. After each beating, I'd grab a pencil and start writing. It was dark in the room, and I welcomed that darkness. I'd cry and hold the steno pad in my lap and let my pencil tell the world what my mother did to me.

Do you know what my lousy mother did to me tonight? She used any excuse to hit me. 1) She found out I lied to her. This I did many times—to placate her, to escape her knowing where I really was. *2) She caught me with a boy*—and that was always the best reason for her to punish me. *3) I talked back to her. 4) She caught me stealing from her purse. 5) One of her friends saw me kissing a boyfriend.* She'd erupt like a volcano, spewing her molten fire out on me.

My mother beat me, and I didn't do anything wrong. I hate, hate, hate her! She hit me on my arm with a strap and I have a welt on it. Just look at the black-and-blue marks. I'd scribble some more. *She detests me and hits me for nothing. Someday someone is going to read this and know what she did to me. I despise her and wish someone would beat her up. She thinks she's a good mother by pretending all of us are to blame for her temper. She's the worst one, and I wish I had any other mother than her.* I'd rant and rave about the injustice, how unfair she was.

All my friends can go out to movies, dances, have friends over, but no one is allowed in our house, so I have to babysit her, stare at the walls, and listen to her in bed moaning and groaning her miserable life away.

No matter who I talk to about the beatings, they don't believe me. They don't know what she does when no one is around. She never appreciates what I do for her. All my mother does is ask for me to do more and more—get her medicine, bring her tea, go to church and pray for her. I'm sick and tired of doing things for her. God, I wish she'd get sick and die.

I'm so mad at my father now. He's away and who the hell knows where. No one has his address because he's living with one of his girlfriends. I'm so mad that he won't take me away from here.

I'm going to get back at my bitch of a mother someday. I'm going to make her pay for what she did to me. As soon as this steno pad is full, I'm going to kill myself and then leave it where everyone will find it and know about the beatings. Although I wouldn't have been alive to witness it, my fantasy was that someone in authority would pick up the steno pad, read in horror what she did to me, and then accuse my mother of murder.

They'd yell at her. "You are a terrible, mean, and evil woman. You caused your daughter to kill herself. You are guilty of severe and unjust cruelty, and now you must be punished. As you kept your daughter imprisoned in this apartment, now you will be imprisoned until you die."

Justice would be served. Finally, she would suffer as I had. Sadly, I would not be alive to see the police take my mother away in shackles. *She makes it look like she's so pathetic so everyone feels sorry for her. But I don't. I know who she is—a wretched, wicked woman.*

I wish someone would punish her like she does me. Let her feel some physical pain for once. I need to find a way to get away from her. I don't know how to do it right now, but I'm going to keep looking for a way out of here or die trying.

16. THE LIBRARY

Forget the men in my life. I have had a love affair I haven't shared with many people. For as long as I can remember, I've been in love with libraries. I'm crazy about them.

I can't remember how old I was when I got my first library card. Maybe ten or eleven. All I can say is that I treasured it—my ticket to all the books waiting for me to read them.

The first library I fell head over heels in love with was in my childhood neighborhood in the Bronx. That one—in a two-story building where the custodian actually had an apartment at the top floor—that's the library I loved the most. I wished I could have lived in that apartment instead of the one I actually lived in. Mine was a tenement apartment with a lot of shouting, anger, and tension in it. My immigrant mother was terrifying. She had fits of unpredictable rage. There were roaches and mice in the house. No one had to tell me we were poor. The neighborhood was also frightening with drug dealers, hustlers, and hookers on the streets. Rumbles between gangs were common with sirens blaring and police cars patrolling the area. I looked for a sheltered place to hide.

The small branch library in the lowly neighborhood where I grew up became my safe place. This was my go-to refuge in my teens. A quiet shelter for my troubled soul.

I'd walk into the place and notice the spiral staircase to the left leading to the caretaker's apartment. To the right was a counter where the books were checked in and out. The rest of the place was filled with large oak tables and walls of shelves stacked with rows and rows of books. I remember being crazy about Eugene O'Neill and his stories. I'd pick up another book—maybe a romance novel—open the pages, embrace it with my eyes, and the book would give me a big hug back. Books. Love. Bliss.

The gray-haired caretaker and I would talk sometimes when he was dusting the shelves or mopping the floor. Joe was about age forty—a tall, thin man. Sometimes his little girl would follow him around. He'd stop his work, pick her up, hug and kiss her. *Oh,* I thought. *So that's what love looks like.* He'd ask me about school, what books I liked, and which ones were my favorites. I drooled with envy that he actually lived in the library. He asked about my family and I told him about my Greek immigrant mother, how strict she was. I wonder if he could sense my unhappy home life because he invited me to dinner with his family. He was a kind man. I regret I felt too shy to accept his invitation. No one in my family ever explained the rules for dinner invitations. I never had any. What should I say? How do I act? Do I wait for others to start eating or can I just dive into the dish? I didn't want to make a fool of myself. Better to decline.

Today, I'd be up those stairs in a heartbeat. They'd have to pry my hands off their door. I'd never want to leave. Not just because of the custodian's generous hospitality. I'd gulp down his warmth towards me like a cup of hot chocolate on a winter night. Oh no, it wasn't just his kind, caring spirit. It was all the books on the floor below which made me want to stay there forever. I wanted to sneak down after the library closed and read them all. They were more than books to me. The texts inside the books were food for the starving emptiness inside me. They were magical friends that could transport me anywhere in the world of words.

In my teens, my mother had erratic mood swings that scared me. I never knew when, like a volcano, she would erupt. I felt fear anytime I was near her. Something I'd say or do would set her off. Usually, she'd catch me in a lie (and I always lied to her). Then she'd give me a whack, a slap or a pinch. The safest go-to place for me to be was the library. My haven, my refuge, my sanctuary.

As soon as I entered the place, I'd take in the fragrance of the books from the shelves—a musty aroma, like an aphrodisiac, a magnet to something inside, hungry and yearning. The silence in the library was a relief, an enormous contrast to my mother's screaming voice at home. My rapid heartbeat slowed down. The quiet felt like a warm security blanket. The books surrounding me were my protective shield against the fearful outside world.

Okay. I'll confess. The library was also the place in my teens where I'd meet my Puerto Rican boyfriends. They'd never get into our apartment. My mother would never allow anyone who wasn't Greek to enter our home—especially, no boys. Even at age sixteen, I was forbidden any contact with the neighborhood boys. She held on to her peasant values, ones from her Lesbos island village in Greece that I never shared. My mother carried those traditions and customs around like a pet animal she thrust on anyone around her—like it or not.

In the warm coziness of the library, I'd sit next to Juan, each of us pretending to read our book. The chemistry of just being next to him made the energy between us sizzle.

When I celebrated my sixteenth birthday with friends at the local candy store, someone told me there was an opening for work at the library. I filled out an application and prayed on my knees I'd be hired as a page. When I learned I got the job, it was the best birthday gift I could have ever imagined. At last I could go to the library for a legitimate reason and get paid for it as well. Now I could say to my mother, "I'm going to work at the library, Ma. I'll be home late."

Over the years, wherever I lived, I found a library nearby to give me comfort, to educate me and broaden my mind. My need for love and kindness didn't stop in New York.

I lived in Los Angeles in the '60s married to a dominating Greek husband. I chose him to escape my mother's control. Sadly, he encompassed all her characteristics: dictated what clothes to wear, how to wear my hair, who to talk with, and what classes to take. He knew I loved the library. He knew my passion for books. He knew I wanted to take a stack home every time. He'd grab my arm before we even entered the place.

"Only one book," he'd say. "You can take out only one book."

After I found the courage to leave him, I met friends who'd drive me to the L.A. Main Library where I'd take out a batch of books to read. Just to carry them in my arms was pure freedom, pure bliss. Love in my arms. I could take out as many books as I wanted without anyone to stop me. I hugged them like they were my babies, all the way home.

Over the years I have had friends and lovers that offered kindness and compassion, but for me, libraries will always be the place where I get the unconditional love and kindness I missed in my childhood. On empty, I get refueled.

Now I live in Oakland. My number one love these days is the Lakeview Library next to Lake Merritt. I'm there so often the staff know me by name.

I may have a biological family in New York, but the library staff in Oakland have been another kind of family, one filled with caring support. They don't have to touch me. Every time I enter, I feel their loving arms around me. "What do you need?" they ask. "How can we help you?" There aren't any books anywhere they haven't found for me. "Don't worry," they say. "We'll get whatever book you need."

They all know my struggles and pain to birth my first book.

I shared my hopes when I told them I'd sent a submission to some agent or publisher.

"How did it go?" they'd ask. "Did they accept your work?"

I'd shake my head no. "Another rejection," I said. "I should get used to it, but it still hurts." I'd get a comforting hug.

"Don't give up," they said.

Then the miracle happened. I recently submitted to a local publisher and was accepted. "Guess what?" I exclaimed. "I'm in, at last. Someone wants to publish my book."

Lakeview Library is where I'll launch my first book next year.

Here's another secret you won't be surprised to know about me. I'm promiscuous. I have many different library cards. There's one for Berkeley, another for Contra Costa County, one for Alameda, and still another for San Francisco.

I have a fantasy that may surprise you: in every new library I look around and take twenty minutes to scope out the place. I want to find some hidden nook among the bookshelves so when it's closing time, no one will find me. I imagine after everyone leaves and the front door is locked, I'd have the place to myself. At my leisure I could roam the stacks and take any book of interest to read. I'd find a comfortable place and put all the books I'd collected all around me—like a warm blanket.

In the morning, the staff would be shocked to find me asleep, covered with all my favorite authors: Hemingway, Faulkner, Kazantsakis—you know, the usual suspects.

When I die, I don't want them to cover me with dirt. I want to be buried with books, the ones I never got around to reading and the ones I want to reread. I could never get enough because there is an infinity of books out there. It would take more than a lifetime to read them all.

17. ALBERTO

We met at the library, where I met most of my boyfriends. Alberto would look at me and smile. I would smile back. This flirtation went on for a few weeks. One summer night as I headed out the door to leave, Alberto asked me if I had time to go out for a soda. I could tell he was nervous. His hands shook as he held the door for me.

We walked to the ice cream parlor a block away. The tables were full so we sat next to each other on stools at the counter and ordered ice cream from the young clerk. Alberto's face beamed as he looked at me. This guy was interested in me. This kind of attention felt new. Even in a crowded room, we created a setting to talk intimately.

"Tell me all about yourself," he said. His eyes held mine. "Anything you want to know about me, just ask."

Alberto's openness was refreshing. Most guys I knew preferred I not know too much about them. They seemed to signal that we keep some distance between us. I didn't want to talk too much about my life either.

"My family," he said, "just moved to New York from Mexico. I have three sisters who all work in the beauty salon down the street from our apartment. Now tell me about you."

"I'm a senior at Walton High," I said. "I live with my sister and mother. So, where do you go to school?"

"I go to NYU," he said, puttering with his spoon in the ice cream and showing his pride in seeking higher learning.

Whenever any man I dated said he was going to college, I was impressed. Anyone who attended college had to be more intelligent and ambitious than the neighborhood guys. College was a magical place, one I wished to attend but couldn't.

"And I major in psychology," he said.

Wow. I was fascinated. My family called me the dummy. In his family I could tell he was the star.

"My father worked on a farm and hated it." He put his spoon down. He'd tell me, "Mijo, don't follow in my footsteps." Alberto grew quiet. "There was never a question about my going to college."

Everyone in his clan was proud of him, and I could see it. I knew his family gave that to him. I yearned to have that kind of encouragement too. Alberto had a confidence in himself that I lacked. And he valued my opinion on anything we spoke about, like theater and music. This felt unfamiliar and wonderful to me.

Alberto was on the heavy side, but his appearance didn't matter. What drew me to this man was how he looked at me. I loved his interest in me as a person, not because I was pretty. He was captivated with everything I said. He listened to me and treated me as an equal. I knew I mattered to him.

We'd go out to coffee shops and talk. No matter what the subject—family, psychology, our hopes and dreams—we would talk and time would disappear. This guy was brilliant. He may not have been physically attractive, but I loved the way he thought and expressed himself.

"You're a bright, beautiful young lady," he would say. "I mean it." He'd kiss my face. "You can achieve anything you want in life."

I hadn't the faintest idea what that might be, but his words melted my heart. We went everywhere, from art museums in Manhattan to concerts at Carnegie Hall. We dined in cafes in Greenwich Village. Alberto introduced me to flamenco music. Each date was an adventure. Everything was exciting with Alberto. He opened my eyes to the world outside our neighborhood, shared his interest in diverse societies and his sweeping enthusiasm to discover new things. He unlocked a part of my brain that had lain dormant. How could I not love this man?

One evening we were walking to my home from the library. We held hands.

"Don't forget," I said. "We have to stop a block from my house."

I didn't want my mother to see me walking with a boy and make a scene. She was now more vigilant than usual, watching my every move. Alberto knew that she was strict and didn't allow me to date, especially if the guy was not Greek.

"Oh, come on," he said. "She can't be that bad."

"Yes, she is," I replied. A silhouette, her dark shadow ahead of me, caught my eye. We both saw her. Uh-oh. My mother's unmistakable form moved toward me like a wild beast. She was headed right at me for the kill. "Al," I said. "Quick. Cross the street."

He ran, but not fast enough. We were caught.

She approached me first with a clenched fist in the air.

"Now you're going to get it," she said. My mother crossed the street to where Alberto was walking. I raced to intercept her just as she grabbed his arm. Shock filled his face.

"You no talk my daughter again, you hear?" she shouted, raising her hand to strike him. "I call police." My mother looked wild-eyed and crazy. Alberto gawked at her dumbfounded, staring in disbelief.

I felt so sorry for him. With all his study of psychology, he had no weapons to deal with my demon mother. I felt certain nothing like this ever happened in his family.

Then I thought, *Where was his courage to fight for me?* All his intellect didn't mean anything at that moment. He stood there immobile, unable to act. I hoped he would stand up for me and be a protector against my villain mother. Yet, I too felt unable to help the situation. I stood there like him, paralyzed with no voice to speak, no power to assert myself. The whole scene felt unreal, like a horror movie with the killer raising a knife to murder someone in slow motion with no one to stop him.

My mother had discovered my secret: I had a boyfriend. This had been my worst fear, my most terrifying nightmare. And worse, she created a scene in the street for everyone to witness. Some neighbors opened their windows to watch the drama. I looked up and saw two women looking at me and laughing, but I couldn't see anything funny about this situation at all.

After that, Alberto and I still went out, but much less, making sure we covered our tracks. Whenever we dated, we'd look behind to see if she was following us. We both expected her to be lurking in the shadows, ready to pounce and pummel both of us. Somehow the encounter with my mother ruined everything.

But he and I were going in two different directions anyway. His path was headed to graduate from college and become somebody. My goals were to finish high school and get a job in Manhattan. He was on an express train, and I was on a local. Still, he had given me a sweet taste of another world outside the Bronx. Sadly, with all his brilliance, nothing he might say or do could rescue me from the world I lived in.

18. A BEATING
IN THE BRONX

The building in the Bronx amid gray tenements lining both sides of the street was my apartment house, 752 Trinity Avenue. This area wasn't just a dangerous slum with drug dealers, hookers, and hustlers. Danger lay within the building where I lived. Danger was my mother.

Whenever I'd come home from high school, I'd go up the stoop, ten steps to the door. Loneliness engulfed me because I was never allowed to bring a girlfriend home with me. Even if they were Greek, my mother wanted to know what island they came from and if their relatives had been on the same boat when she came to America. All my friends were either Puerto Rican or Cuban. I wasn't attracted to any Greek guys. Our apartment was like a fortress with no one to be trusted outside our walls. You needed a Greek password to cross our threshold.

Faded gold mailboxes, some of them broken, lined the side of the entry to the hallway of our building. I'd climb up the stairs carrying my textbooks. The hallways with cracked paint on the walls held dark shapes that felt scary. At any moment I expected a shadow to turn into a man who would attack me. I don't know which I feared most—the stranger who might creep up and strike me from behind or what lay ahead in my mother's apartment.

I gripped the banister as I got closer to the fifth floor and apartment fifteen. Like an animal expecting to be devoured by a predator, I'd sniff the air to see if it was safe to enter the apartment. I never knew what to expect when I opened the door. Her rages terrified me. I yearned to find a way out of this hellhole.

My pudgy mother sat in the kitchen dressed in an old, drab, faded housecoat, her wrinkled face all drooped, worried, and weary. I felt powerless to cheer her, to take away her despair. Her robes reached to the floor but didn't touch her run-down slippers. She looked weak and pathetic. As a child I had loved her and looked for ways to bring happiness into her sad life. The world she lived in was her small bedroom. Few entered, few were allowed to leave. I felt sorry for her.

As an adolescent, my feelings were changing. I felt like Cinderella, with my mother the wicked stepmother who never permitted me to leave the house. She just assigned me endless cleaning duties. Like the torn dishrags in the kitchen, I felt worn and wrung out.

"You're late," my witch-mother would say as I entered the door.

"I was at my girlfriend's house," I'd reply, backing away from her.

She'd roll her fingers into a fist. "Liar," she'd accuse. "I saw you from the window. You were at the corner talking to those filthy Puerto Rican boys. I saw everything. Don't try to lie to me."

And, of course, she was right. I always lied to her. Outside of the apartment, I hung around with the boys in the neighborhood. I loved being with my Puerto Rican and Cuban sweeties and took every chance to sneak out of the house to be with them. I always cautioned my boyfriends when they'd walk me home. I told them about my mother's vigilance.

"Drop me off a block from my house in case my mother's looking out the window," I'd say. They'd look at me with disbelief and laugh. I assumed everyone in the neighborhood knew about my mother's paranoia and wild rages.

"You come home now!" she'd scream at me from our tenement window. My mother had a reputation. Neighbors kept their distance.

The most recent heartthrob in my life at that time was Tomas, someone new I met at the local library. He was tall with dark brown eyes, thick, black, wavy hair to his shoulders, and soft lips I loved to kiss. He was a freshman at a local college. I always went for guys who were both Latin and intellectuals. I hoped their smarts would rub off on me. Tomas talked to me as an equal, sharing what he learned in his English Lit classes on Shakespeare, taking me out to jazz concerts and the theater in Manhattan. It meant a great deal that he saw something in me beyond my looks.

"You'd love this English Lit class I'm taking," he'd say enthusiastically. "We're talking about Shakespeare's *Hamlet*." Tomas would put his arm around my shoulder and squeeze me tight. We often sat in the library, reading our books, holding hands, gazing at one another. I was in love.

After being within the closed-in walls with my mother, Tomas was a breath of fresh air. His intellect contrasted with my mother's illiteracy. His interest in the world was wide open, 180 degrees opposed to my mother's narrow and rigid Greek one. He was generous with his affection and told me he loved me. He looked into my eyes when he spoke, and smiled and touched my face with tenderness. My mother barely looked at me and then only with cold eyes. Her hands would strike and hurt my face. I guarded myself against the buildup of rage that led to beatings. Tomas took me out to many cultural events, dances, films, and theater. My mother's world focused on the church and little else. He contrasted with everything that happened within the walls of my apartment. At home I was an imprisoned slave. With Tomas I had freedom.

To get out of the house, I'd say to my mother casually, "I'm going to study with a friend at the library." She would hesitate for a moment and fix me with her look. Then she'd give her okay because I'd used the key word—*library*. I flew down the stairs two at a time, out the door, into the street, and on my way to my sanctuary, the library, to my Tomas, a brief pass to freedom.

At home cockroaches crawled all over our kitchen walls. At the library, precious books covered the walls. My home had loud shouting and chaos. The library had silence and order. It became my shelter, a quiet safety zone. Whenever I entered, I felt I was in a sacred space with a feeling of spirituality surrounding me. I never wanted to leave my refuge, the library.

———

As I grew older my mother increased her vigilance. I was sixteen now. She had begun to stalk me, following me to the library, looking to see who I sat with and whether I had a book in my lap. Wherever I went, she was not far behind me. Once, I saw her in the stacks, wearing a stained housedress. Where did she sneak in? She shuffled toward me in her floppy old slippers. She saw me studying with a girlfriend for an exam the following day. Whew, I got a free pass on that particular night.

On another winter evening after the library closed, Tomas and I both wanted to go to our respective homes and get warm. We walked close together with his arm around my waist. At times we stopped in a doorway to kiss.

I had an eerie feeling we were being followed. I slowly turned my head to look. There I saw my worst fear: my mother. About a half block away was her unmistakable form. This chubby little lady with a dark shawl over her head moved her small feet rapidly like a military tank coming closer and closer for the attack. I thought, *this is it. This is the end.*

I grabbed Tomas's hand. "Run!" I shouted. "It's my mother and she's going to kill me!" I sobbed, crying hysterically. I could not breathe. My knees shook, and I felt nauseous, about to throw up. My head was swimming, and I thought I'd pass out. I gripped Tomas's arms to steady me. He grew pale with a look of discomfort. He dropped my arm. He had never seen me in this state.

"I have to split," he said. "I have an early class tomorrow." He took off running. As his body receded down the street, I saw my mother's form looming larger and larger moving rapidly toward me. Tomas was gone. I knew I was alone in this. Now what do I do?

The only place I could think of for temporary refuge was the local community center. This was an afterschool hangout where teachers supervised teenagers who played volleyball and card games. That night the center was the place I ran to for help and protection from the imminent punishment from my mother's usual assault weapons: the coat hanger, the large wooden spoon, and that damned iron cord.

I pushed the door open and looked around. The only adult I recognized was a tall Chinese counselor I'd seen before. She came over to me.

"What's wrong?" she asked. I was crying so much I could not reply.

She put her arms around my shoulder and walked me to the director's office. He was a short, bald, brown-skinned man. He sat behind his large oak desk and played with a pencil, twirling it around his hand. I told him about my mother's stalking. He listened as I described how terrified I felt. While I sat there blubbering, someone knocked on the door. The young man walked in.

"Your mother is downstairs and said you should come home now." This is the end. I thought. She's going to kill me.

I looked at the director with desperation. "Please help me," I pleaded.

He called over one of the female counselors—a young, petite, Puerto Rican woman in her thirties. "Walk home with her," he said. "She's afraid of her mother. When you get back, give me a report of what happened."

We went down the stairs and I was relieved to see my mother had left. The counselor asked if there was any other place I could stay that night. I told her my father lived about a mile from our place. He was the only other relative around.

"Let's try your father's place," the counselor suggested.

Every step walking there, I prayed he'd be home.

Please be home, Pop, I implored God's help over and over again. *I need your help. Just this once.* We climbed up six flights to his apartment. I banged on his door with my fists. No one answered. I banged again so loudly neighbors opened their doors. A young Latina woman peeked out from behind her door.

"I don't think he's home," she said. "I saw him go out tonight with his girlfriend."

What did I expect? That he'd be there waiting like a good father, to be there for guidance and protection when most of my life he was gone? I really hated him at that moment. *You're a lousy piece of shit, Pop,* I thought. *I need your help and you're not here when I need you.* I had no other choice. What else could I do? I had to go home to my mother.

———————

The counselor and I left and walked in silence to my apartment. It was late, and the streets were dark and empty. The gray tenements all around the street closed in on me.

Then I saw a figure in the distance. My mother stood in front of our building. Even from afar, I could see her eyes were blazing with rage. She appeared like a black menacing creature—tense, ready to pounce, focused on the kill. Despite the cold wind, my armpits were wet with sweat. I stood there, like a deer facing the headlights, unable to move.

My mother waddled down the street toward me. She stood in front of me and the counselor. Her whole focus was on me. She raised her arm from her black coat, like a film in slow motion. Her hand lifted and moved with full force. Her open hand whacked me on the right side of my face. The slap stung my skin like needles. The force of her blow pushed me to the ground. *Crack.* Her foot struck my back. I scrambled and got off the ground, crying. The counselor stood there in shock. My mother grabbed my arm and pushed me toward our apartment building.

"Move," she said grabbing my arm. "You're going to get it!" she said, spitting out her words at me. "Oh, yes, now you're really going to get it." She was on a roll. "You listen to me good," she shouted. "You no talk boys no more!" *Smack!* "You no leave house except for school!" *Kick!* Like a dictator, my mother issued her commands and ordered my punishment.

I turned my eyes to the counselor. She just stood there speechless. Her eyes held a look of fear and disbelief. My mother continued her assault on me. The woman's hand lifted to her own face to protect herself. She expected my mother to strike her too.

"I have to go home now," the counselor said with a shaky voice.

She turned and walked up the street. I felt a dreadful despair. Where else could I turn to for help? No one could protect me from my mother.

"*Tha se skotoso.* I'm going to kill you, just wait," my mother warned. I believed her.

———

I'd see Tomas at the library occasionally. We'd go out for a soda and talk. After my mother chased us down the street, everything changed and I just saw him once in a while.

One night when I returned to the community center, the counselor who walked me home called me over.

"Come into my office," she said. "I want to talk to you about something." She had a file with my name on her desk. "About that incident with your mother a few weeks ago," she began. I nodded. "Well, we'd like to help you with the problem with your mother. We want to refer you to a social worker."

I laughed. What she didn't know was that I had sought advice from teachers, friends, relatives, and even a Greek priest about my mother. It was a joke talking about her. At any given time and place, I could just start up a conversation with any stranger about her abuse. I wore my mother around my neck like a snake, hoping someone could help me remove its strangling grip.

Most people didn't really care to hear my sad story. They had their own problems. I could not conceive of anyone being able to help me. I took the piece of paper offered by the counselor with the name and address of a clinic and the name of the woman I was to speak with there. *Okay*, I thought. *I'm willing to take the train from the Bronx to Manhattan to meet with this woman, just once, to check her out.* I held no hope that she could help me. After that last beating in the street, I had given up.

Still, I clutched the paper in my hands. I wondered if there might be something different about this woman. I did not know it then, but that small piece of paper with her name on it was the turning point in my life. The name on the paper read Emily Lou Jackson, Social Worker.

19. MISS EMMY LOU JACKSON

Her office was small. Just a large oak desk and a couple of chairs crowded one side of the room. A diploma hung on the wall. I faced Miss Jackson across her desk, squirming in my seat. Everything in the room felt strange and unfamiliar. I didn't want to be there. She looked calm and in charge.

"My name is Emmy Lou Jackson," she said. "I'm the director of this clinic."

She was about medium height, a bit on the plump side. Her navy tailored suit with a white silk blouse looked formal. I noticed her eyes were dark blue and her blond hair dropped to her neck. Miss Jackson's face was pale, with clear skin, and she spoke with a slight Southern drawl. Not someone I felt I could relate to. In fact, I didn't like her.

"Do you want to tell me," she asked, "why you are here?" She wanted to hear my story. Then she would refer me to one of the several social workers in the clinic. So I told her about my Greek mother, how hard I tried to please her, and that I could not take her rages, beatings, and screaming at me any longer.

"I've tried to do what she wants," I said. "Be a good daughter. Nothing works. No matter what I do, she finds something wrong with me. No one is allowed in our house. She even follows me in the street to see if I'm talking to boys. I can't change anymore. Now she needs to change."

She looked at me. Her eyes never left my face. Usually anyone I told my story to showed some reaction—a look of shock, disbelief, some sympathy. Miss Jackson's face showed no emotion. She just looked at me, made notes on her yellow legal pad with her fountain pen, and listened to everything I said.

I wasn't use to this kind of response to my Greek drama. I wondered what she had written on that page. "How long," she asked, "do you think it will take to change your mother?"

She held her pen, poised over the legal pad. "Oh, about six months," I replied. Six was a good enough number, I thought. I watched as she wrote all this on the yellow pad. After a while, she closed the pen, held it in her hand, and then placed it on the desk. A full minute passed.

"I've decided," she said, tilting her head, "not to refer you to another social worker. I will see you myself." Her reply scared me. I hadn't expected that response. What had I said that made her decide to see me? She looked strong, not like someone I could manipulate or control. I didn't like that. I couldn't read her face. I liked the attention and sympathy others gave me after hearing all the terrible things my mother did to me. Miss Jackson was different from anyone I'd ever met before. There was no impressing her or making her feel sorry for me; she'd never say, "Oh you poor thing," and pat me on the head. Something about her calm coolness frightened me. I didn't want to come back and see her again.

Did I really want help? I pretended to want help with my problems with my mother, but some part of me knew I enjoyed the drama of my life. The issues with my mother were familiar parts of my world. These problems had been with me for a long time. Who would I be without them?

"You're sixteen," Miss Jackson said. "We require a parental signature as a legal measure."

I got up to leave. Now I had a good excuse not to come back. My mother was illiterate and couldn't even sign my report cards. I had to forge her signature. I could never tell my mother I sought therapy because of her abuse.

"It's no deal," I said.

In our Greek culture what was all-important was appearance. Everything should look normal to outsiders. No one must know what lies behind that curtain, what's kept secret behind it. No one must know the truth. God forbid! If my mother knew I told others that she beat me, my punishment would be even worse.

"My mother is an immigrant and can't read, write, or speak English." I shook thinking of what she'd do to me if she found out I had spoken to anyone about her outrageous behavior. "She would forbid me to come here if she knew I told anybody what was going on at our house."

Miss Jackson sighed. I remained standing. She toyed with her fountain pen, twirling it around in her hand. We waited together in silence. I wondered how she would respond.

"Sit down," she said quietly. "I'll make an exception in your case and waive the signature requirement." I sat down. This woman was going to work with me whether I liked it or not.

———

The following week I missed my appointment. I just forgot, or so I told myself. This therapy business felt a bit overwhelming. What would be required of me? How was I supposed to behave? Despite my fears, I felt there was something Miss Jackson could do to help me, so I returned. When I did show up for the next appointment, we talked about the one I had missed.

"I don't blame you for not keeping our appointment," she said. "This is not going to be an easy journey you are undertaking." She looked at me with those deep blue eyes of hers. "You won't be alone," she said. "I plan to be there with you every step of the way."

I felt uneasy. Could this lady see something worthwhile in me, someone worth saving? My feelings toward Miss Jackson changed in that session. Despite her professional cool demeanor, I felt her kindness. My body relaxed into the chair. I believed she cared about me. I never missed another appointment.

Each week she had a fresh yellow legal tablet on her desk, and her black fountain pen lay right next to it, in readiness to write.

"What would you like to talk about?" she'd ask.

Then Miss Jackson would open her pen and start writing in her tablet.

The topic each week was the same: my mother, what she did, how she terrorized me, and how I always lied to get out of the house and away from her. Miss Jackson never tired of hearing the same story. Once, after I told her about yet another beating, she put down her pen, pushed the tablet to the side, and looked squarely at me.

"At what point would you defend yourself from your mother's beatings?" she asked.

I had no answer. I didn't know what to say. As a good Greek daughter, I'd been taught never to strike back at my mother. I'd surely go to hell for that. How could I defend myself?

"Well," she asked, "Would you defend yourself within an inch of your life?"

Within an inch of my life—what life? Wait a minute. What was she asking me?

"Oh, yes," I replied. "Of course, I would protect myself within an inch of my life."

Miss Jackson looked at me, pushed back her chair, stood up in front of me, and repeated what I said. There was a long silence before she spoke again.

"Did you hear yourself?" she asked. "Did you hear that you would tolerate your mother beating you within an inch of your life?"

How could this question be answered? What does "an inch of my life mean"? Whose life was she talking about? Certainly not mine. I did not believe I had a life worth living. Naturally I would allow my mother to beat me, not just within an inch of my life, but to my death.

The feelings I had toward my mother were so full of hatred and rage that I believed I deserved to die. Kicking my corpse, she'd convince everyone I was evil and deserving of death. I held onto a fantasy that someone would discover the diary next to my body and be shocked at what they found. Then they would arrest my mother for murder. Ta-da! The police would handcuff her and take her to jail. "Guilty as charged, murder in the first degree," the judge would say and sentence her to die. Yippee!

But that was not what Miss Jackson was asking.

Why didn't I fight back, hit her, grab her throat and squeeze it? Why didn't I push her, give her a punch right back? I could not do any of that. My mother and I were in a dance of death, tangled in a twisted rope of rage and pain. This was the only reality I knew. My life felt worthless.

I felt enormous guilt. I hated my mother with every cell of my being; I often wished she would die. Those feelings were mixed with immense pity for her. We were poor. We were alone. No one understood us. I concluded I was the cause of all the misery in her life. The beatings were punishment I justly deserved.

All these thoughts rushed into my brain. The old ways of thinking were that I lied, stole, and hated my mother; therefore, I deserved punishment. The new ones were that I had a right to defend myself and protect myself from her wrath. Could there be another way to escape my mother's harsh treatment? How would I do that?

20. REUBEN

I met Reuben at a neighborhood party in an apartment near Prospect Avenue. My girlfriend and I were both seniors in high school. Gloria knew a lot of guys from Cuba who liked to throw parties with Latin music and all the rice and beans you could eat. Reuben stood near the corner of the room with his plate full of food. He paused between bites to look at me. I looked back at him too.

"Haven't I seen you in the library?" he asked.

"Could be. I work there as a page," I replied, checking out his dark brown eyes and his wavy black hair. Not very tall, about five foot seven, a bit taller than my five foot, three inches. He wore a navy blue sports coat that looked expensive. Maybe cashmere? I guessed he was a little older than me, maybe early twenties. I found him attractive.

We made small talk. I liked working around books, I told him. His family came from Cuba, he said. I told him I went to Walton High School and asked him where he went to school.

"Fordham University," he said. "Majoring in chemistry."

Oh my. I was impressed. I loved guys with mental power that went to college. I was attracted to the brainy hombres.

All I wanted was to graduate from high school and get any kind of job that paid money, hopefully decent money—enough to get me out of the Bronx.

Reuben asked for my phone number. I told him we had no telephone in my mother's apartment. He took out a piece of paper and pen from his pocket and wrote down his number.

"Call me," he said placing the small piece of paper in my hands. He held my fingers for a long moment. I liked that.

"I live with my parents," he said, withdrawing his hands from mine. "If you call when I'm out, they'll give me your message."

I went to the table and fixed a plate of red rice and beans and came back to where Rueben stood. "Do you like opera?" he asked. "*Carmen* is playing at the Met, and I'd like to take you to see it."

Gee, this guy had good looks and class. I didn't know a thing about opera. I'd never been interested because it seemed like just a lot of loud singing on a stage. But I wasn't going to let that stop me from going out with Reuben and seeing what kind of man he was.

I was ready to learn something about anything, including opera. And if Reuben wanted to teach me, I was eager to learn from him. I'd have to dress up, maybe borrow one of my sister's fancy dresses. I felt excited, like Cinderella going to the ball.

———

My immigrant mother would have a fit if she knew Reuben was Cuban, not Greek. That night I told her I was visiting a sick girlfriend. I rushed out the door before she could see my outfit. Reuben and I met at the Jackson Avenue train station.

On the train, Reuben explained what the opera *Carmen* was all about. A gypsy has a flirtation with a guard. The guard falls passionately in love with her and leaves his military post.

Carmen becomes bored with him. She falls for a matador and leaves the young guard. Devastated by Carmen's betrayal, he stabs her to death. The end. I was thrilled to hear the story and couldn't wait to see it on stage. But I didn't want Carmen to die. I loved her spirit.

At the theater, the usher showed us to our burgundy velvet seats. I wondered how much our tickets in the orchestra cost. I looked around and saw there wasn't an empty seat in the theater. I noticed some of the women wore gowns and glittering earrings while their escorts wore formal tuxes. Where had I been? Why hadn't anyone told me about opera? Reuben took my hand. He whispered in my ear that I looked beautiful. By the time the orchestra played the overture, I was spellbound. Everything about the setting felt special.

The curtain came up with men and women in costumes all singing a foreign language. I didn't understand their words, but that made no difference. I felt entranced by the melodic arias sung by the lead performers, especially Carmen. She captivated all of us with her passion. She didn't care what anyone thought of her. I admired her wild spirit. Secretly I wished I could be that brave and daring, and not care about anyone's opinion. My eyes darted everywhere to capture the drama before me, and Reuben sitting next to me was the cherry on a sundae. He smiled and squeezed my hand.

Later we went to a café and had hot chocolate and a slice of layered coconut cake. We shared the dessert from the same plate. I'd never seen a cake like that in our Greek household. We poked at the cake and sat and talked about his job at a local drug store. Reuben was fascinated with chemical solutions to people's ailments.

"The pharmacy is not far from the library," he said. "I'd like you to drop in and see me sometime. I don't think my boss would mind."

Reuben talked a lot about himself, the classes he was taking, and how he looked forward to finishing school and getting a job as a pharmacist. Everything about him impressed me. I felt lucky to be with him. When he kissed me goodnight, it was a two-second peck rather than a deep, lustful kiss. I wanted something more fervent from him, but guessed Reuben was a little shy—the reserved type. I knew he liked me, and for the moment that was all that mattered. I thought so little of myself I dared not ask for more than he gave.

He asked me out again to go a movie. When he hugged me goodnight, I could smell his aftershave. Later I'd have that fragrance on me too. We went to concerts. He took me to movies. We went to the zoo. Part of my infatuation with Reuben was that he opened me up to the cultural life of the city. That new world appeared suddenly at my feet. I'm not sure whether I was more taken with his college intellect or his cultural interests, not to mention the money he spent on our excursions. Whatever it was, I felt flattered that he'd found an interest in me. I was in awe of him. We both liked movies, Latin music and food. We had long conversations together.

We went out every week. He always embraced me and told me I looked beautiful. After dating for several months, he surprised me by giving me his school ring. Now I knew our relationship was serious, and that he cared about me. The Fordham U ring meant we were officially going steady. I felt so proud to be his girl.

———

After we had been dating for almost a year, he took me out for pizza one night because he had some news to share. It was 1950 and the Korean War had begun. This was an episode in the Cold War between South and North Korea, but America was using it to fight communism and the USSR. I was sad to learn he'd been drafted and would have to go overseas. Even though Reuben was in college, he had to leave school and everything behind, including me. In a few weeks, he said, he'd be leaving for the army.

The day he left, I rose early and went to the train station with Reuben and his parents. I'd met them before, and even though they spoke mostly Spanish, they understood I loved their son. He looked so handsome in his army uniform. I hated to say goodbye.

"I'll write you," he said, as he stepped onto the train.

Within a month I got my first letter from him and immediately answered it. I poured my heart out in my letter. I told him how much he meant to me and how I longed to see him again. I missed him terribly. My mother never suspected my affair because I'd get to the mailbox before her. I'd tear open his letters, eager to hear how much he'd missed me. But his responses were impersonal compared to mine. "The weather here is cold and wet," he'd write. I didn't care about the stupid weather. Why didn't he tell me he loved me, and that he couldn't wait till we were together again?

We corresponded like that for several months, me writing fervent letters of longing for him, and him returning vague brief replies. I couldn't figure out what was going on with him. I wanted him to write how he ached to see me again.

Sometimes I'd go to his parents' home. Even though they spoke little English, they welcomed me. I would share that Reuben had written me and hold his letter to my heart. They were pleased to know how much I loved him.

Several weeks passed without a letter from Reuben. I wrote to him but got no replies. I felt concerned. Was Reuben all right? So again I went to his parents' home. His mother answered the door. She stood there and looked uncomfortable. "*Ay, Dios,*" she said, her hand to her face.

I looked beyond her. There he was at the dining room table—Reuben. He was in uniform. I felt a punch to my stomach, stunned at what I saw. Everything felt jumbled inside. I was shocked to see him and confused that I didn't know he was coming home. Why hadn't he let me know? Why did he stop writing?

"What the hell," I said. "Reuben, when did you get home?" He wiped his mouth with a napkin and looked down at his plate. He wouldn't look at me. I walked closer to him and stood at the table.

"About a week ago," he murmured. I couldn't believe it. I felt crushed at his response.

A week ago? I couldn't believe he hadn't written me that he had a leave coming up. And now that he was home, why hadn't he made an effort to see me? What was going on? I felt anger coming up from my stomach to my throat.

"We need to talk," I said tersely. I wanted some explanation.

He got up, grabbed his jacket, and we left the house.

We went outside for a walk. "I can't believe you didn't let me know you were home," I said.

"I didn't have time," he said, putting his hands in the pockets of his jacket. I reached into his pocket for his hand, but he neither welcomed mine nor resisted. "Besides," he said, "how was I supposed to let you know? Your mother wouldn't have allowed me in your house."

"You could have stood outside our apartment," I argued. "You could have written a note and given it to some kid on the street to knock on my door and give it to me. I'd have been down the stairs in a minute. What happened to stop you doing something, anything to see me?"

I wanted Reuben to come to my house and break the goddamn door down to see me. What the hell was going on? Where was his *cojones*, his courage, his willingness to do anything to contact me? I couldn't believe he had made no effort to reach me.

I thought he loved me. I loved him. Reuben's actions told me he no longer had any feelings for me. Every word he said stung me. I had taken for granted the love I felt was there. I had no choice but to believe it was over between us.

He wrote me several letters after that, but I never replied. What for? If he didn't think I was worth the effort to try to see me on his furlough, then I felt it wasn't worth my effort to keep the relationship alive. In fact, what relationship did we have? There was none. Still, I thought of him constantly, wept with grief, and wondered if he ever missed me. I felt injured, obsessing over what went wrong between us. I spoke to my therapist about Reuben. She encouraged me to move on. Not easy for me to do. I dated other guys, but still thought about Reuben.

A year passed. Then I got a letter from Reuben in the mail. Could we meet so I could return his ring? He was no longer in the army. He was back at school. He said we could meet at the neighborhood candy store.

I was distraught. All my wounded feelings from his rejection came back with a vengeance. If Reuben was through with me and wanted his ring back, he'd get it— right in his face. But I worried how it would be to see him again. How would he look? Could I contain my emotions? Would we embrace? I knew I still had feelings for him.

Before we met that evening, I wanted to look appealing, so I borrowed my sister's pale blue sweater to wear with navy slacks. She trimmed my hair. Before leaving the house, I put a dab of her cologne on my neck and wrists. I knew I looked good.

When I walked into the store, two guys at the counter gave me a low flirtatious whistle. I saw Reuben sitting in the back. As soon as he saw me, his eyes lit up. He got up and walked over to me. I could see he was glad to see me. He took my arm to offer a seat next to him. His eyes never left my face. I felt numb.

Reuben ordered sodas for us. He fidgeted in his seat. I took his ring out of my pocket and put it on the table. He held it in his hand and twirled it around. Did he want to give it back?

He stared at me and cleared his throat. "You look more beautiful than I remember." He laughed nervously. Our sodas arrived, and he played with the straw in his glass. "This is strange to admit, but seeing you now, I feel like I'm falling in love with you all over again." Really? *Too late*, I thought. *You lost someone who adored you.* He looked like a sad puppy wanting me to pet him, to take him into my arms. I said nothing.

The jukebox was playing Billy Eckstein's "I Apologize." Someone kept feeding the jukebox and playing the song over and over again. *Great*, I thought. *Keep playing it.* I wanted Reuben to hear that song. I wanted him to get how hurt I had felt when he rejected me. The lyrics were painful. Billy sang, "If I caused you pain, I know I'm to blame. Must have been insane, believe me. From the bottom of my heart, dear, I apologize."

Reuben smiled. "You know, I really do apologize for everything. I should have stayed in better touch." Was he joking? There had been no emotional connection at all. I got up, left my soda on the table, and walked away. I didn't look back. Now our relationship finally was over.

I had to step back and take a look at my pattern with boyfriends. I always went after the Latin good-looking guys who went to college, like Reuben.

I didn't understand Reuben or how to connect with him. I'd like to have found a way to get him to share his feelings. Above all, I wished I knew what happened to him in Korea.

I wanted the desire and passion of Carmen. Maybe his Catholic beliefs held back his emotions. All I know is I wanted some shared feelings between us. Perhaps I was too much Carmen for him?

But it was too late for anything he'd try to offer. I was done. Korea had changed him. I couldn't understand it. He couldn't explain it. So I moved on to another boyfriend.

21. A MEETING WITH
MY MOTHER

Showdown time. As I climbed the five flights of stairs to apartment fifteen, one step at a time, the hallways were dark and smelled like a bar after closing—stale smoke mixed with beer, whiskey, and urine. The stairs were cracked with age. I was sweating, not just because it was late June, but from fear of facing my mother. I'd been her caregiver for too many years. I never knew when to expect her attacks and rages, only that they were going to be swift and painful. At eighteen, it was time to stand up for myself, to request more time to be with friends and have more fun.

To observe my mother, you'd think she was a nice, harmless old lady. Innocent. Kind. Not a mean bone in her body. None of that was true. My mother's rage and bitterness leaked out in my presence. The dark side of her personality was hidden behind our apartment walls. No matter how I tried to explain to my girlfriends, teachers, and even the local priest how tough it was to live with my mother, no one really understood. No one except Miss Jackson knew how bad it really was. She knew the truth.

I was eighteen years old in the 1950s, and my mother monitored my every move, especially on weekends. Tomas, an old boyfriend, called to take me out. He remembered my birthday and invited me to celebrate with a pizza dinner and a dance at the Palladium ballroom, where the mambo and cha-cha were all the rage. I was excited and wanted to party with him. But how was I going to get out of the house? My mother could not bear to be alone, and I felt it was my duty to be her companion. Actually, I felt more like her hostage.

Miss Jackson and I rehearsed over and over again my speech to my mother. It went something like this: "Ma, I'm eighteen years old now, and I would like to have more freedom. I'd like to go to the movies, the church dances, and go to dinner with some of my friends."

It sounded like a reasonable request any normal young woman might make, but I knew my mother would fight it tooth and nail. She needed me to be with her in her misery. I was braced for her finding any reason to refuse me. I expected her objections.

"You want to go out?" she'd ask. She'd stand up and give me that look, the Greek dagger one, as though I had asked her if it were okay for my boyfriend to sleep over, for me to use drugs, or to have sex orgies in the house. She would play her ace, the guilt card. "You can't leave. You need to stay home with me. Can't you see I'm ill? Do you want me to die? It is a daughter's duty to be home when her mother is sick and alone." Then she'd always throw out the zinger: "Do you know how I almost died giving birth to you? How I've suffered to raise you?" And the final dictum: "No, you cannot leave the house." She would point her finger. "Go back to your room." In the past, I obeyed because I was terrified of what she might do to me if I didn't.

It would be easy to just leave if I had my own key to the apartment, but my mother held the only key to the place. If one of us was out, we needed to knock on the door to get in. Once, when my mother was napping, my sister snuck into my mother's purse to get a copy of the key made. Unfortunately, for some reason, it did not work.

There was no Society for the Prevention of Child Abuse in the fifties. And if there had been, I could not have reported her for cruelty; my guilt would have been too great to bear. The truth was I believed I deserved the beatings. I got no allowance, so I stole change from my mother's purse and felt I deserved her punishment. I knew my father favored me over my mother. The combination of pity and vengeance toward my mother was too complex for me to deal with. The other reason I felt I deserved the beatings was that I hated my mother with every fiber of my being. I wanted her to die. There was great guilt in my murderous feelings toward her.

And finally, as much as I hated my mother, down deep inside I loved her. I was sad that she had such a miserable life, that she had married the wrong man—my father, who drank and abandoned her. Many times, sitting at the kitchen table as she prepared a meal, I urged her to fix herself up.

"Hey Ma," I'd say. "Why don't you fix up your face, go out and visit your Greek lady friends in the neighborhood? Get out of the house for a while?" But she was afraid to leave her familiar surroundings. In her home my mother had control of her universe.

That steno pad with details of the beatings filled up rapidly. Page after page I'd write of the pain, the bruises, and the killer rage I felt after each punishment. When there was no more room to scribble, I gave my therapist the whole book. She looked at me knowingly, and quietly asked what my plan was. "Iodine," I said. That is what my girlfriends told me would kill anyone who took it. Truthfully, I didn't want to die. I wanted my mother to die—or just disappear and leave me the hell alone. My therapist stood up and faced me. "I will not allow you to harm yourself," she said firmly. "Do you understand? No more."

I entered the dark apartment to confront my mother with my plan to leave that prison cell that evening and every week, to be let out for a few hours of fun and freedom. I felt like David facing the giant Goliath, trembling with fear and terror that I'd be annihilated. My mother was seated on an old worn-out couch, the Greek Bible in her lap. She had a frayed blanket over her legs. She wore a dark brown dress down to her ankles and a black shawl over her shoulders. Her gray hair was pulled back in a knot. The living room wall was covered with icons of Christ on the cross, Holy Mary holding the baby Jesus, and other biblical images. The paint was peeling in some places on the ceiling and, from the corner of my eye, I saw a mouse run across the room under a chair.

"Ma, I need to talk to you about something," I began.

My mother looked up at me, and I could see from the tightness around her lips and her piercing eyes that she was prepared with her emotional weapons, aimed right at me—the Greek crazy logical arguments why I could not leave the house for any reason whatsoever. She took off her glasses. "What is it you want?" she asked.

"Now that I am eighteen, I want to go out on weekends. In fact, I want to go out tonight, for my birthday." I could not believe I was actually saying these words. My mouth was dry, and I felt weak against her arsenal and the Greek army behind her. I could see her mind working overtime, her energy in high gear, ready for attack.

"Didn't I let you go out last week?" she retorted. "Didn't you to go to the movies with your girlfriend a week ago?" Then the killer punch to the stomach: "Now you want to go out again?" There she sat on her high throne, the judge who had just found me guilty of greed and selfishness. She continued her attack sprinkled with guilt. "Can't you see I'm sick? I need you to stay home and take care of me." Pointing her finger at me for emphasis, she shouted, "You are not leaving this house," Then, the final order: "Take off your dress clothes. Get back to your room."

It was as though she had X-ray eyes and could see that underneath the coat I wore was a black silk dress. It was one I'd taken from my sister's closet that was tight over my ass and made me look sexy. As I stood up to leave, I saw the mouse scurry under my mother's chair. Good, I thought. You keep her company. I'm leaving this hellhole.

"I'm not staying home with you," I said, quivering inside, pulling the coat around me for protection. "I'm going out tonight for my birthday."

She continued shouting curses and threats at me. "Why don't you leave and go live with your no-good father?" she yelled. "Let him worry about you." I knew no matter what she threw at me, I had to go. I had to leave, despite the fact I was petrified of the consequences.

My legs were shaking when I got up and walked to the door. Even though it was only a few feet away, it felt as though I were climbing Mt. Everest. The door weighed a ton. I turned the doorknob to leave the apartment. As I slammed the door shut behind me, I could still hear my mother screaming as I took to the stairs.

"You had better come back here now," she hurled at me, a last threat of violence. "God will curse you if you go!" It was the Greek arrow of doom struck straight at my back.

But as frightened as I was of the consequences of defying my tyrannical mother, the two years of solid therapy had given me strength and courage I did not know I had. I now could take those first shaky steps away from her and release the control I'd allowed her to have for most of my life.

Closing the door that night was one of the hardest things I had ever done. I had confronted my mother, defied her, and left her alone with her personal demons.

I wish I could say I had a good time on my birthday with Tomas that night. But all I could think about that evening was what scary things would await me when I banged on my apartment door and once again had to face my mother.

Surprisingly, I took another giant step closer to the door to freedom sooner than I expected. This time the rehearsal to leave my mother was close to the last act.

22. BUILDING COURAGE

I could talk to Miss Jackson about anything, even though some subjects like sex were harder than others to discuss. At seventeen, I knew a lot about kissing and petting, but nothing else.

Neither of my sisters ever spoke to me about this subject. And my mother wouldn't dare say a word about sex. That subject was taboo. My mother didn't have to say anything; we all knew what she thought about sex and men in general.

"Men just want one thing," she'd say grimly. "They take it. Then they leave you."

No one had ever taken time to explain to me how a woman's body works. I knew nothing about sexual intimacy and ways to avoid having a baby. Miss Jackson patiently explained what a normal mother would tell a daughter about menstruation, intercourse, the use of prophylactics, and other ways to prevent pregnancy.

"Isn't there such a moment as now or never?" I asked Miss Jackson, covering my mouth with giggles and embarrassment. I sat fidgeting in my chair, talking about something I knew nothing about and yet wanting to get some answers.

"Me and my girlfriends talk about feeling pressured to do it, have sex with the guy in the heat of passion. What if he makes us have sex, so do we just let them do it?" I asked. "And what happens if I miss a period?"

One of my boyfriends had been pressuring me to have intercourse. This was an important topic. Turning him down was getting more difficult. If I didn't do it, I'd lose him for sure.

"Come on, baby," he'd purr in my ear. "I'll pull out before I come. It will be all right."

I loved him like crazy and enjoyed his tender kisses. But the threat of getting pregnant, confessing that sin to God, and facing my mother scared the shit out of me. If my mother beat me for talking to boys, I knew she'd surely kill me for losing my virginity, not to mention getting pregnant with a Puerto Rican, no less.

Miss Jackson responded to all my questions.

"Do I have to do it?" I asked. "What if they're like right on top of me with their thing out?"

"The answer is no," she said firmly. "There's always time to go down to the corner drugstore and get some rubbers." Her honesty always floored me.

We also talked about money. I'd just gotten my first job out of high school at a Manhattan bank; I couldn't wait for payday.

"What do you plan to do," she asked, "with your first paycheck?"

Dumb question. "Spend it, of course," I answered. "I want to buy shoes and stuff."

"That's okay." And then she paused and pierced me with those blue eyes of hers. "What about saving some of it?" she suggested. "You work in a bank. Why don't you open a savings account? Each payday put a few dollars of that money in savings before spending it."

Savings? What the heck is that? In our home money was scarce. Every month my mother would wring her hands with worry. "The rent, the rent!" she'd wail. "How will I find money to pay the rent?"

I opened up a savings account. Seeing my money grow each payday became exciting. I liked the feeling that this money was mine. Money made me feel strong. Saving money became a regular lifelong habit. I never ever wanted to be poor like my mother.

Each payday I proudly told Miss Jackson how much I saved, how much I had in my account. She explained that money was also available to spend when needed.

"The money is there for you to use in emergencies and for you to enjoy."

As my savings account grew, my respect and love for Miss Jackson grew as well.

23. IMPORTANT TESTS

When Miss Jackson and I had been working together for a year, I started to wonder whether there was more I needed to learn about myself. Had I changed? Was I different from when I first walked into her office? How could that be determined?

She had mentioned there were services the clinic could provide, like psychological tests. This appeared to be the right time to take a battery of those exams. Miss Jackson agreed. Arrangements were made for me to meet with a psychologist in her office who specialized in testing. The results would be forwarded to Miss Jackson. She and I would then discuss what they determined.

It took several visits with the psychologist to complete the tests: the Rorschach, the Sentence Completion, the Draw a Person, and the MMPI, a personality inventory test. The tests were interesting, and I answered all questions honestly. I scribbled my heart out on the one called Sentence Completion. I held nothing back.

After a few weeks, Miss Jackson and I sat together, and she explained what the results of the tests indicated.

"Please tell me," I asked eagerly, "what's in the report?"

"I can't tell you everything that's written in the report," Miss Jackson said, holding a sheaf of papers on her desk. "I can tell you this, however. The tests show you are experiencing a great amount of stress. Your current environment is not safe."

No kidding. Tell me something new. I don't remember much of the rest except the last part when she said, "The examination concludes that you shouldn't live with your mother. It is dangerous for you to be there." The report continued, saying I was experiencing a great amount of anxiety and depression in the current living situation.

"You know I can't leave," I said to Miss Jackson. "My mother couldn't handle it. She would die, and it would be all my fault."

I actually believed my leaving would cause my mother some terminal condition. Every illness my mother had, she blamed on me or others in the family.

Miss Jackson put the report to the side of her desk and then gave me a homework assignment to consider.

"Why don't you make an appointment to meet with your mother's doctor and ask him what would happen to your mother should you leave."

This assignment made me nervous. What would her doctor tell me? Not knowing made me even more anxious. I made an appointment with my mother's doctor the following day.

———

Dr. Morris had an office on Grand Concourse. My whole body shook with anxiety in his waiting room. I knew he would tell me not to leave, that if I did my mother would surely die. The six-foot doctor towered over me. Dr. Morris had thick white hair with a gray beard and kind brown eyes.

He brought me into his spacious office with large windows and a garden view.

"Have a seat," he said pointing to the chair in front of his desk. "How can I help you?"

"I'm thinking of leaving home," I said. "What will happen to my mother if I move out? Will she get sick and die?"

"Well, she's getting on in years," he said, scratching his gray beard. "You know she wouldn't like you to leave." He continued thoughtfully, "She'll feel bad about it, but your mother won't die." His honesty impressed me. As I left his office, I didn't feel happy about the consultation, but I did feel great relief. If I left, my mother would not die.

A few weeks later, I made plans to consider the idea of leaving. But first I needed to take practice steps to reach the door. Giant steps. I needed courage to face my mother. I needed guts to grab the door to freedom.

24. THE DOOR
TO FREEDOM

The church in our area sponsored dances. Anyone and their family were welcomed. I wanted to go to all the dances, but was rarely allowed to. After my eighteenth birthday, I felt I had the right to go out more. Miss Jackson encouraged my being more assertive, to ask for what I wanted. And that night, I wanted to go to the dance.

I went to Alexander's Department Store not expecting to find the right outfit for the church event. But I did. On a clearance rack, I saw a black velvet turtleneck top with a skirt to match. I hurried to the fitting room and tried on the blouse and skirt. The skirt caressed my backside just right, a perfect fit. I touched the fabric and put the garment to my face. The cloth felt like a baby's skin, so soft and velvety. *Oh yeah*, I thought. *Wait 'til the guys see me in this.*

The only obstacle to get to the dance was my mother's consent. Dealing with her felt like banging my head against a wall, repeatedly. Now my mother sat in her usual stuffed chair in the living room, eyeglasses falling off her face, her black shawl around her shoulders. The Greek Bible lay open in her lap.

Her bleak mood cast a cloud of darkness into every crevice of the room. I went into my bedroom and put on my undergarments, the half-slip and new silk stockings. Then I put on the velvet top and slipped into the skirt, feeling like Cinderella ready to go to the ball. Now I had to pass my mother's scrutiny. Would she give me her stamp of approval?

I needed to hide my velvet outfit. If she saw what I was wearing, she might disapprove. With a coat, I covered the dress. Better to disguise the evidence. Then I would approach mother on her throne.

"I'm ready to go to the dance, Ma," I said, my voice quivering with anxiety. "Don't worry. I won't be late." She looked at me and nodded.

Her cold eyes pierced me. Up and down my mother X-rayed me. I made for the door. All I could think was, *Let's get the hell out of here fast before she changes her mind.*

"Just a minute," she said. "Come back here." She took a long look at me. "Take off your coat." Up and down her eyes went over me. "I want to see what you're wearing to the dance."

I hesitated. Once she saw the outfit, I predicted she would disapprove. Then my mother would order me back to prison. I had no choice. I took off the coat.

"Tsk, tsk." She shook her head from side to side, frowning. "No, you can't go out with that sleeveless dress." She was adamant. "It's not proper. Sleeveless. Take it off and put on something decent to cover your arms."

I closed my eyes. I didn't want to hear her. All I wanted was to wear the new outfit to the dance.

"Find another dress," she said. "You can't wear that one to the dance."

"There's nothing wrong with the dress, Ma," I groaned. I wanted to choke her, kill her right there. I gritted my teeth. "I don't want to wear anything else." For once I took a stance.

"Then you can't go out," she said.

I looked at her face. Her lips were tight, determined. The Almighty One had spoken from her high throne. The tension between us felt like two boxers in the ninth round. No matter what I said, I knew there would be no way to make her budge. I was down for the count. There were other times I could get her to move, to bend a little, debate, or negotiate. But now she refused to let go even an inch of her rigid position. Her tone was firm and final. I felt defeated.

"Take it off." Not just off with my dress, but off with my head.

I should have known better. I should have known what she'd say the moment my coat opened and my mother saw my slinky velvet outfit. Why didn't I think to grab some rag from the closet, wear it, and put my outfit in a shopping bag? The witch would grudgingly have given her okay. Then when I got to the dance, I'd go to the ladies' room and change into the velvet outfit.

Wearing the new dress had clouded my logic. It was my fault for not using a strategy to outsmart her. There was no probability that she'd let me ever wear something revealing to leave the house. Not a chance. My mother declared my outfit as enticing to all the men at the dance, and that is exactly what I wanted—for all the boys to gravitate toward me and my beautiful outfit. No wonder she wouldn't let me wear it. And how many dances had her parents allowed her to go to from her little village? None. Of course I couldn't dress up and go out. She never did.

"Did you hear me?" she said, her voice raised in anger. "Take off that dress."

I didn't move. I just stood there. My mother put the Bible down, got up and moved toward me. She raised her hand toward my face. Her hand closed into a fist. *Here it comes*, I thought, *another beating.* Instead, the fist remained steady.

"If you go to the dance tonight, don't come home," she said in a cold voice. "Go and stay with your rotten father."

Don't come home? Go to my father's place? Was she crazy? My father was never home. Where else could I go?

The clock on the table *tick-tocked* like a hammer on my head; I needed to make a different move, do something else. This was the final round. The silence felt like a bomb about to explode.

I got up. My body was drenched with sweat. My armpits, my legs damp with sweat. The time had come. I sighed.

"Okay," I said with calmness and finality. "I'm going to leave."

I walked to the door. My legs felt like a ton of lead. I could hardly move. Yet my mind was going crazy. Could I really do this? Was I actually leaving the house? My mother got up and followed me, her hand pushing at my back.

"You get out of here and don't ever come back!" she screamed, moving close behind me to the door. All this was said in Greek, of course.

Here it comes, I thought, *more shit.* Would she strike me from behind? Maybe she'd follow me into the street? Another big fight for the neighborhood's entertainment; they'd just love it.

"You tell your father to keep you." She stopped in the hallway. Her arm rose toward my face. "I don't want you here anymore."

I turned away to avoid her slap. I pushed open the door and flew down the stairs. I did it. I got out. But could I stay out? That would be the hard part.

———

Before I did anything else, I needed some spiritual guidance. I walked several blocks to the church to get some advice. There were lights I could see in one of the rooms. I knocked at Father Anthony's rectory. He opened the door a crack to see me.

"Who is it?" he asked. Father Anthony was a short, thin, gray-haired man. He wore a long, black, embroidered garment. He knew me and we had spoken often. "Oh, it's you," he said, smiling. "What is it, my child?" He opened the door fully and invited me in. Sobbing, I explained my dilemma. I wanted to go to the church dance.

"She said if I go to the dance then I should leave home and go and live with my father." I wanted to go to the dance, but I didn't want to live with my father. "I'm looking to you," I said to the priest. "I need your guidance, your blessing. Tell me what to do."

I stood there waiting for his response. The priest had heard my story before. I'd knocked on his door many times asking for advice about my mother. He had always sympathized with her, explaining how hard it was for her to raise four children alone with no financial support from my father. Father Anthony had urged me to pray and have compassion for my mother's situation and remain her dutiful daughter. "Be patient," he would say. "Your mother is depressed and needs your prayers and understanding." Then he'd send me away.

"What shall I do, Father?" I repeated. "I'd really like to go to the dance. But my mother forbids it. She threw me out of the house."

He closed his eyes. Was he praying? He touched the crucifix on his chest. Then he looked at me.

"This is not easy for me to say to you," he said. His face looked determined. "I think you must now leave your mother's home and go and live with your father."

I was eighteen now, not the fifteen-year-old who had

come to him before. This time was different. This time he saw me as old enough to deserve a more mature response.

I couldn't believe it. I had Father Anthony's blessing, at last. There was a God. Father Anthony walked me to his office. He let me use his phone. Miraculously, my father answered.

"Pop," I said. "Mom won't let me go to the church dance. She's kicked me out. Can I come and stay with you?"

"That woman is crazy," he said. "Of course you can come here."

Although I went to the dance, my mind was focused on the high drama I'd left behind with my mother—leaving home, and now going over to my father's place. The excitement I felt in my bedroom showing off my fancy outfit disappeared. Now that I had Father Anthony's blessing, together with Miss Jackson's encouragement, I couldn't stay at the dance. In a short while, I left.

I went straight to my father's house. He had made up the couch with sheets and a cover in his living room. I put the velvet dress on a chair. My father gave me a pair of his pajamas.

"It's late," he said with a yawn. "We can talk about this tomorrow, but if you want to stay here you can." He said he had a room he'd fix up for me.

My sleep was restless that night. What was going to happen tomorrow? How would I tell my mother what the priest had said? Would I tell her? Would she even believe me? What would she do when she heard I wasn't going to stay home anymore?

Who was I kidding? Inside I knew I wasn't ready to leave. The idea was still too new for me to handle. My ties with my mother were strong and intricate. I'd need more practice to build more confidence to stand up to her.

The dilemma I faced was not whether I should leave my

mother. Everything pointed me to the door. It was whether I could actually leave her and not return. Despite the key to my father's apartment being safe in my pocket, I knew I wasn't ready to sever ties to my mother and move to his place quite yet.

To separate from my mother was more complex than I realized. We were enmeshed, twisted together in a sick way. I needed practice facing my Goliath mother again and again before I felt strong enough to get to open the door to freedom and leave for good.

I went back home the next day and told my mother what the priest had said. Her face fell. She turned pale. For once I held an ace in my hand. For once, someone in power had become an ally. The door to freedom looked possible. I hoped to reach it soon. One giant step after another.

25. LEAVING HOME

Surprises scared me, but Miss Jackson had taught me the importance of planning ahead. We devised a way that I would leave my mother's apartment. I had taken practice steps. I'd worked hard to get to this point. Now all our sessions were focused on my leaving home. At age eighteen, I'd earned the right to leave. I clung to Miss Jackson's guidance like a life raft.

"I don't know if I can do this." My insides rumbled. "I'm so scared."

The key to my father's house was secure in my pocket. He said he had room for me, but could I actually move there? The problem wasn't that I wanted to leave my mother. It was how to leave this woman and make it stick? I would visit my father and stay overnight like a trial run, taking practice steps away from my mother's place. Now I was prepared to take all my stuff and move to my dad's apartment. I had enough rehearsals. It was time.

I wanted to *live*, but my mother was suffocating me. Although I had doubt this scheme would work this time, every cell of my being wanted to leave now. I had to get out.

I could never confide in my sisters my plan to leave. They depended on me to take care of mother. Neither of them would support my departure. It wasn't in their best interest. Once I left, I also expected my sisters to come after me, to try to convince me to come back home. They might be nice to me and even make me feel I mattered.

Sure. Of course they would. Their main worry would be that they'd lost their mother's caretaker. Now that I would no longer be there and available, they'd be pissed. Who would run all her errands, listen to her endless complaints? These were tasks I was doing now. My mother didn't speak, she screamed. Neither of them wanted that job. I had to pretend I planned to stay.

———

Each evening after work as a typist in a bank, I'd return to my mother's home. I carried out the garbage, cleaned off the table, and washed the dishes. I did whatever my mother asked. It wouldn't be long now. Soon I'd be in my father's place.

My mother's apartment felt like a familiar hell I was accustomed to. Despite his drinking and many girlfriends, being at my father's place, in contrast, gave me a feeling of great relief, it was a potential sanctuary. My mother was strict, rigid. My father was lenient, laid back. I was between two worlds. One I knew very well. The other one offered me an unknown freedom I desperately wanted. It might not be perfect, but I knew my life would be more peaceful at my father's place. I could no longer kid myself. I wanted a new life at my father's home. I inched away from my mother's apartment toward that door to freedom.

Early each morning I grabbed a handful of clothing from my room and brought them to my father's apartment. I dumped dresses on my new bed. I left a few things in my drawers. My bras were worn out, the elastic frayed. I had several pairs of shoes—one pair of flats and the two dressy pairs of pumps. I grabbed them too and put them in a shopping bag. The skirts and blouses in my closet I just carried over my arms. I must have looked strange to anyone seeing me walking down the street with shopping bags and clothing over both arms. Then I'd run to the subway and go to work in Manhattan. If my mother noticed, she said nothing. She wouldn't believe I could ever leave her. I could hardly believe it myself. But my eye stayed fixed on the door, the door to freedom.

———

After a few weeks, the closet was empty and the drawers were bare. The room just held the bed. Now I needed to deal with my mother, and tell her I was leaving home.

That evening I was alone with her. She sat in her usual place, an old upholstered chair with stuffing coming out of the sides, with knitting in her lap. The needles *click-clicked* as she knitted away, her nervous fingers moving in and around the ball of wool.

This was it. My moment. My heart pounded so loud I thought she could hear it. Come on, come on. Let's get this over with. Help me, God.

I faced my mother. She looked up from her knitting. I took the gold house key I now had from my pocket and placed it on the kitchen table. *Plunk.* The key seemed to glow on the dark wood. I slid the key toward my mother. My thoughts were a jumble. I couldn't believe it. I was actually doing this.

"I'm leaving now," I said. "I'm not coming back."

She put her knitting down and stood up. She looked at me. Her face turned red with rage.

"What did you say?" Her eyes pierced me. Her hands turned to fists. "You're leaving?" She spit at me. "I curse you." She waved her fist in my face.

I stood still as she hurled her threats at me. Her face was inches away from mine.

"You are the worst of my children. How I wish I'd never borne you. Only a whore would leave her mother's home."

Though I had expected them, her words stabbed my heart. I could hardly stand to look at her.

I didn't want to leave this way. Just once couldn't she give me her blessing? Couldn't she send me off with her good wishes? Instead my mother's words felt like rocks being thrown at me. Ducking to avoid getting injured didn't work. I still got hit.

I moved toward the door. My body felt heavy and bruised as though I'd been beaten. When I turned that handle with all my might, I knew this was it. Time to leave home. Finally.

The click of the door behind me started me down the stairs. Then the door opened again. I looked up. My mother stood at the railing, her face contorted and full of rage.

"Drop dead!" she shouted down at me.

Where the hell had she learned that? Her final insult, so American. I choked up, swallowing my tears. She had to have the last word. Running down the stairs, feeling the fresh cool air from the street, I knew I had already left her behind.

26. A NEW LIFE

I savored my new independence at my father's place. Freedom to go out, whenever and wherever felt like heaven.

Over time, my mother mellowed. When I visited my mother, and she seemed pleased to see me. I'd leave a few twenty-dollar bills on the kitchen table. She grumbled in her usual way, but I believe she held a new respect for my courage to leave.

Occasionally, I'd take her to the local park and buy her an ice cream on the way home. We had a different relationship now. With my new freedom, I felt more compassion for my mother.

Miss Jackson and I continued our work together until I was nineteen. She was leaving the clinic to get married. She'd lost weight and began wearing colorful dresses. She looked beautiful. I was jealous of her fiancé. Although I had eagerly wanted to leave my mother's home, I never wanted to leave Miss Jackson's office. In our last session together, I tried to hide my feelings from her. I squirmed in my chair. I avoided looking at her. She wouldn't let me do that.

"We've done a great deal of work together," she said, looking me straight in the eye. "Is there anything you want to say to me?"

A flood of feelings came over me. I wanted to bolt from the room. How could I begin to tell her how much I'd miss our time together, how much she meant to me? Tears came streaming down my face. I could not hold back my feelings for her. I walked over to her desk and put my arms around her.

"I love you," I said, my voice cracking. "You know that, don't you?"

She put her pen down next to the yellow tablet. "Yes," she said quietly, "I do."

27. MY FATHER'S HOUSE

When I moved to my father's apartment, I noticed the biggest difference focused around sound. I was surrounded by a hush of silence. No screaming, no shouting, no Greek drama. There was an absence of fear. The only sounds I heard came from the street. Cars honking. Children's voices. "Throw me the ball!" I heard someone shout. I noticed how peaceful I felt. I loved the serenity of my new home.

The usual anxiety when I woke up at my mother's wasn't there. When I came home at night, I no longer wondered what kind of mood my mother would be in. The chains were broken. I was free.

When I lived with my mother, I gave her my whole paycheck, minus just the carfare I kept for myself. At my father's, I got to keep half my salary, though he charged me $25 a week in rent. After years of absence and irresponsibility, I felt he owed me big time, not the reverse.

Then there was father's girlfriend, whom I disliked and mistrusted. She was kind of a floozy. Fanny and my dad had met at the local bar, which was not surprising. From my bedroom I could hear them stumble in late at night, drunk and knocking over the furniture as they got to their bed. Then the sounds of their lovemaking kept me awake through the night.

Okay, I was jealous of her. The part of me that wanted my father all to myself had trouble sharing him with his girlfriends.

I spoke to Miss Jackson about Fanny, how I suspected her of stealing things from my dresser. Whenever anything was missing or misplaced, I blamed Fanny. I suspected she went into my room when I was working and took my things. When I couldn't find my earrings, I knew she was the one who took them. I would swear to it. After all, she had a key to the apartment.

I discussed this with Miss Jackson who'd helped me leave my mother's home. I'd continued therapy with her to deal with my adjustments to living with my father. Now I had new problems to deal with.

"You know, your suspicions may be correct," Miss Jackson said, "but I doubt it. It seems to me the issue has to do with love."

Her pen hovered over the yellow legal tablet that matched her blond hair. I'd seen her do this many times in other sessions. She leaned forward in her chair and looked at me. I knew she wanted me to pay attention. She was about to say something important.

"The love your father has for you is different than the love he has for Fanny. It's not less, just different."

I didn't like what she said. Not a bit. However, I had to believe her. Despite my trust in my therapist, I could not accept that my father could love us both in different ways. I didn't want to share my father with anyone, especially Fanny. No matter what Miss Jackson said, I still hated that bitch-girlfriend of his and wished my father would kick her out.

Even though I had a Greek boyfriend, Sotiris, stationed in Korea, I continued to date Eddie, a cute Puerto Rican sweetie from the neighborhood. We'd meet at my father's home to listen to music, talk, and kiss. Boy, did Eddie know how to kiss. Where no one was allowed to visit in my mother's home, my father welcomed all my friends. He even allowed this when he was out. Still, something didn't feel right.

My father had a habit of walking into my bedroom early in the morning without knocking. My bedding would be scrunched around and my nightgown up to my neck, leaving my half-naked body exposed. Dad claimed he had the right to enter my room to wake me up. I asked my therapist for her advice.

With Miss Jackson's support, I was able to ask my father to knock before entering. Not easy for me to do. After all, it was his apartment. The look he gave told me he didn't like it, but he reluctantly went along with my request.

"You know," Miss Jackson said, making sure she had my attention, "it's against the law for a father to have sex with his daughter."

Where did that piece of information come from? Had she picked up something from my unconscious to bring to the surface, to keep me alert?

Did Miss Jackson see something suppressed from my past that I had not acknowledged or revealed? Undoubtedly.

I was my father's favorite, the chosen one for his affection. When I was a teen and we'd go out to a movie, we'd hold hands. Not as father and daughter, but as though we were boyfriend and girlfriend. Miss Jackson accurately picked that up.

Now I felt uncomfortable. Things didn't feel right.

The new living arrangement wasn't as wonderful as I'd hoped it would be. I noticed changes in me I couldn't figure out. I didn't know what to do. So I did nothing.

My father became critical of me. He would not tell me directly what bothered him. However, one morning from my bedroom, I could overhear him complaining about me to his girlfriend.

"She's lazy," he said. "She doesn't clean the house or mop the floors." Then he added, "The rent she pays doesn't even cover the food she eats."

All he said felt hurtful, but it was true. I hated house-keeping and dusting furniture. My father expected me to keep the house clean. That's what good Greek daughters did. Household duties. I never learned how to do that. Neither of us felt satisfied about our living arrangement.

He had good reason to complain that dating, going out with friends, and partying were my only interests. Now I wondered whether I should leave his home and find a more comfortable accommodation, but where else could I live? Forget about returning home to my mother. That option never came up for consideration. Miss Jackson and I discussed other places I could go. "There are hotels for women in Manhattan," she said, but the expense would be greater. I didn't like that. Rooming with other strange women did not appeal to me either. Better, I thought, to stay put. I'd clean the house, even though I didn't want to.

Sotiris had a leave coming up. I'd wait and see how that relationship developed. Perhaps he might be the perfect ticket to freedom. The fantasy of marriage to a Greek man seemed the perfect solution to my problem. How could I know what horror lay ahead?

28. EDDIE

At eighteen I dated a lot of different guys, but Eddie, my dark-eyed, Puerto Rican boyfriend, had a special quality about him. This guy knew how to kiss. He was six foot two, with smooth, cocoa-colored skin and thick dark hair. We'd met at a neighborhood party. Someone put a record on with Latin rhythms, a bolero. Eddie held out his hand to me. This guy knew how to dance. He knew how to hold me just right. When we danced, he held me close to his face, his soft skin on mine. I could smell his fragrance, and it went all the way down to my belly. He walked me home after the party and lightly touched his soft sweet lips to mine. I was hooked.

One cold winter morning, we met for coffee in a café close to the train station. I was on my way to board the Lexington Avenue express train to my dead-end typist job at a Manhattan bank.

"Don't go in today," he said, smoothing my hair with those tender hands of his. "Let's just hang out together." Eddie didn't work, so his time was totally free.

I laughed. Every time Eddie touched me, my body tingled. The warmth of our bodies close together could distract me from any obligations. Being with Eddie made me just want to kiss his tasty lips and forget about anything else, including going to work.

"What are you saying?" I asked, melting into his arms. "You're suggesting I play hooky and not go to work today?"

What an outrageous idea. Not to go to my boring, dull typist job in a windowless room with a hundred other women banging away on their typewriters? Instead, spend the day with my gorgeous, cocoa-skinned boyfriend? No competition whatsoever.

"Yeah," he said. He pulled me closer, his warm lips kissing me gently on the cheek. "Come on, you don't want to work today, do you? You really hate that place."

He was right. My jobs were meaningless and empty ones where I filed, or stood at the mimeograph machine making copies. They were shitty jobs where I wasted away at typewriters that *click-clicked* in cramped quarters with other faceless robots, selling my soul, and for what? I'd get up each morning, go to work, come home, eat, wash up, fall into bed, get up, and do the same thing over and over again. Eddie's offer came at the right time, just what I needed to escape my dreary monotonous life.

So just like that, I decided not to go in that day. I found a pay phone and made a quick call to my supervisor. I said I was sick, which was sort of true. This job did make me sick to my stomach. I needed a break.

Hand in hand, like two kids on a field trip, Eddie and I ran to the train station. Breathless, we boarded a car packed with commuters, all going into Manhattan to their own private prison jobs. We were squashed in together and stood close, our arms entwined, his tall, lean body close to mine. Being near him, my heart played bongos in my chest.

Then a voice inside growled, *What the hell are you up to? You're going to get fired from the bank and then what are you going to do?* I'd be broke. No money coming in. Nothing. Forget getting anything from my father, and it might take months before I'd find another dull, boring job.

Blah, blah, blah, I didn't want to listen to any of that monkey-talk chatter. I wrapped my arms around Eddie's waist. This was the place I needed to be and nowhere else. Taking a day off to be with him, away from the hassles of work and home, felt like a gift I deserved.

We got off at Times Square station and jumped into a sea of people, all going to work. And there we were, Eddie and I, playing hooky. We stopped to look at the skaters at Rockefeller Plaza as they glided around the rink to music, like a performance just for us. Then our feet took us to Radio City Music Hall. Patti Page was the headliner on the marquee.

"How much do we need to get in?" I asked the cashier.

Eddie took out some bills from his wallet, and I put a few more into his hand. We pooled our money and got tickets. We entered the darkened theater just as the burgundy, velvet curtain went up.

The orchestra was playing something upbeat. Rows of beautiful dancers in sequined shorts lit up the stage. They all moved and kicked up their shapely legs in unison. I forgot about anything outside our cocoon. Being there with Eddie holding my hand as I held my breath, far away from the cold workplace, felt like a dream.

My eyes stayed riveted on the stage. Patti Page came on wearing a filmy, long, white gown and sang, "How Much is That Doggie in the Window?" The acts went on and on—acrobats, jugglers, and magicians. Eddie squeezed my hand. We looked at each other and giggled. We were in a world neither of us wanted to leave. We were the last stragglers out of the theater.

Later, Eddie bought me a hot dog and spread relish and mustard on it. We took turns taking bites out of it. We hovered close to one another to keep warm.

Now we needed to go home. We headed for the train station. Back on the train, we still clung together, not wanting to have to separate. I hated to leave him. We were both sad. At my stop, we both got off the train.

We stood close, his arms around me. He looked at me and smiled. His face came close to mine. His soft lips kissed my eyes, my cheeks. He traced the outline of my mouth with his tongue. We kissed for a long time, our bodies intimate and warm. People smiled watching us, but I didn't care.

The next day, I dreaded going to work. I stood at my desk. I could see Miss Fitz, her back ramrod straight, expecting me to make up for the previous day's missed work. She gave me that knowing look when I sat at my desk and uncovered my typewriter. I couldn't hide the joy I felt inside. I stared down at my keyboard.

"Feeling better?" she asked towering over me.

"Oh yes," I replied, running my fingers over the keys of my typewriter and holding back a smile. "Much, much better."

29. THE PRESSURE COOKER

I learned to cook from my father. His apartment was on the sixth floor of a tenement in the Bronx. The kitchen where we had our meals was small. My father had owned restaurants in the past, so he knew how to put a spread together. One evening my father surprised me. He came home with a box from an appliance store. I couldn't imagine what the box contained.

"I bought a pressure cooker," he said. "We're going to try this."

Oh hell, I thought. Any new appliance scared me. This was in the mid-1950s, and pressure cookers were the newest kitchen gadget around. The thought of using one terrified me. My eyes got big. I didn't even know how to cook with a plain old aluminum pot, let alone something dangerous like a pressure cooker. No. Not for me. And my father didn't know how to use it either. *Oh, please take it back*, I thought. *I'll never use that thing.*

I'd heard horror stories of women forgetting to wait until the indicator dropped before opening the lid, only to have the contents splattered all over the kitchen ceiling and walls. It was too dangerous for me to try. Forget about it.

"Pop," I said, "I don't think I can use that thing. It scares me—and it feels too newfangled. Can you take it back?" The old aluminum pots and pans were the right way to cook a meal.

But my father insisted. "We can learn to use this together," he said. He got the small booklet out and said, "Why don't we make a meatball dish? Look, we have all the ingredients. Let's just try it." I didn't want to try it. *Can't we just open up a can of spaghetti?* I wondered.

We took a look at the recipe together.

Meatball Stew—a meal in a pot.

1 pound of chopped meat
1 egg, lightly beaten
2 slices white bread, soaked in water and squeezed dry
2 tablespoons minced parsley
1 teaspoon Worcestershire sauce
2 cloves garlic, minced
2 tablespoons olive oil
2 carrots, cubed
2 medium potatoes, peeled and cubed
½ cup beef stock
1 bay leaf

Combine meat, bread, egg, sauce, parsley, and garlic. Add olive oil to pot. Form into 2-inch meatballs and brown on all sides. Add carrots, potatoes, stock, and bay leaf. Close cover and bring to pressure. Cook for ten minutes.

———

We emptied the refrigerator, brought out all the things to put in it, made it into golf-ball sizes, and put these in the pot with—and this was the important part—enough water to cover the ingredients. Then we screwed the cover on the pressure cooker and waited for the black button on top to rise. When it did, we lowered the heat and timed it for ten minutes until the dish was done. Only ten minutes?

I couldn't believe any dish could be done in such a short amount of time. When the time was up and the button went down, my father opened the cover and there was our dinner—fragrant meatballs. Surprise! I couldn't believe it worked. We brought out our plates and scooped the meatballs onto them. We dipped rustic bread into the sauce until our plates were clean.

Gradually I gained courage to make a spaghetti sauce from scratch. My father helped me cut the onions and garlic, add the canned tomato sauce with a bay leaf, and put it all in the pressure cooker. In five minutes, all done. I couldn't believe I could ever make a dish from scratch. Boiled rice and Campbell's canned soup were the only dishes I felt I could handle.

Confidence in the kitchen took a while. Reading the recipes and following them was the key to my success. I challenged myself to try new and different dishes like a beef stew, one of my favorites in the new cook book.

I just loved cooking with my dad, my partner in the kitchen. He always applauded my efforts and would encourage me to try something new. Whenever I took a risk and prepared a meal, he was generous with praise. "Bravo!" he'd say. "You're learning to be a good cook."

30. SOTIRIS

What I noticed first was his sleek, black convertible parked on the curb as my mother and I entered the church dance hall. Later, he told me he'd borrowed it from a relative. I watched him get out of the car: dark, wavy hair and dark eyes, short and stocky, he wore a tan sport coat with navy slacks. I'd seen him in the neighborhood, but lately he hadn't been around. I had heard his family moved to New Jersey.

Sotiris had a cigarette in his mouth. I liked that—someone sophisticated and sexy with a car. That's what I wanted.

That night, on one of the rare occasions she left the house, my mother had agreed to go to a church dance in Manhattan. The musicians were lined up on the stage with their musical instruments—their bouzoukis, tablas, and clarinets. The male singer stumbled around the stage half-drunk. They were ready to start the usual first dance, the Kalamatiano, where all the Greeks get up, join hands, and move to the sounds of uplifting music. *Opa*!

Forget the music. My eyes were searching for the guy with the car. Where was he? Had he left? Then I spotted him at the bar getting a beer. I wanted him to see me, to find me attractive, to ask me to dance. We locked eyes and I smiled.

He walked over to me and asked, "Don't I know you?" He checked me out from top to bottom. "Are you from Trinity Avenue?" His eyes were dark brown, his hair thick and black. He was a little taller than me, and round about the middle. I held his eyes.

"Yes," I said, looking at his mouth and wondered how he kissed. "I still live on Trinity Avenue."

"Can I buy you a beer? You want a soda? My name is Sotiris." In Greek his name meant "savior." Perfect, I thought.

"No, no," I said. "That's all right." I didn't want to look too greedy.

"Let me give this beer to my father," he said. His eyes checked out my breasts. "I want to talk with you."

Oh, yes. I wanted to talk and do anything he wanted with me.

He asked for my telephone number. We had none.

"Err . . ." I faltered, embarrassed because we were poor, and could not afford a private telephone. I searched and found a pencil in my purse. "Here's the number." I scribbled it on a napkin. "The pay phone is in the hall. Just ask for apartment fifteen." I prayed he'd call soon.

I don't remember much of what we said that night. All I could think of is how much I wanted to see him again, to have him take me somewhere in his car. Anywhere.

At last, I thought, *my ticket to freedom. Sotiris. My Greek savior.*

He did call, and I invited him over to our apartment. He came to the house one evening and spent all his time in our kitchen talking with Dora, my sister. I was angry. Had he come to see me or my sister? When I confronted him later, he told me he was nervous and didn't know what to say to me.

He told me his family had just moved from the Bronx to New Jersey. His parents owned a dry goods store. They had a little money. He had no job, but he was looking.

I'd just graduated from high school a year earlier in 1954 and I was working a boring job as a typist in a bank. With my low self-esteem, I felt lucky to have a job. I'd applied to get a better job at the United Nations, but they wanted college graduates.

On dates, he took me to the movies, and later we kissed in his car. I let him touch my breasts and he put his hands under my panties. We went no further. My mother had instilled in me the importance of being a virgin when I married. "Men just want one thing," she warned, "and then they leave you."

"You feel so good," he said. Sotiris held me close. His attention felt like love to me. We continued to date and did everything intimate except intercourse. I wanted to do all I could to please him. *This is it*, I thought. *This is the one.*

I met his parents and his younger brother, Andrew. His father was a big man with a beer belly. His mother was petite. They owned their own home—a normal family. I wanted to be a part of my vision of an idealized family—parents, a home, and a father who worked—nothing like mine.

One night Sotiris took me out to a seafood restaurant. As a surprise, he ordered oysters. "Here," he said, stuffing one into my mouth. "You'll like it." I tried to eat it but gagged and spit it out into my napkin. He got angry. "Everyone likes oysters," he said, annoyed with me. "What's the matter with you?" Control was one of the signs I didn't recognize. I had to agree with his likes and dislikes. I saw no other options.

We went out to a café for breakfast. The eggs I ordered were too soft and runny. "I can't eat these," I said.

"There's nothing wrong with them," Sotiris said. "Just eat them." I swallowed the eggs and my resentments. I disregarded the signs that showed something was wrong with this guy. I only wanted to see the good parts.

He told me he liked to draw. "Someday," he said, "I want to be an architect."

"Let me help you," I responded eagerly. "We can move to California. I'll get a job and help you through school."

"You'd do that?" he said kissing my face.

"Anything," I said. "Just get me out of New York."

We had been dating for about three months when he got notice that he had to go to Korea. I was devastated. He'd be gone for a year, he said, maybe more. All my dreams had to wait until his return.

Every weekend after he left, I'd visit his parents' home in New Jersey. His mother would welcome me with open arms. "Oh," she'd say. "You're here. I'm so happy." I was the daughter she never had. She was the loving mother I always wished for.

While Sotiris was away, I fell in love with his mother. Anna was a kind woman who cared about me. She'd look at me when I arrived and say, "Are you all right, honey?" She'd take my hand. "Was the bus ride long? You must be tired. Come into the kitchen. I'm making lamb stew for dinner." I'd watch her chop the onions and garlic, humming and clearly enjoying my company. "Here," she said, giving me tomatoes to dice for the stew. "You help me." It was an unexpected occasion to see my mother cook, her depression kept her in bed. Now I had this dear lady who openly enjoyed cooking and sharing her feast with me. I adored her.

"Is that a tear on your blouse?" Anna asked. "Take it off and let me fix it." I'd watch her thread the needle and carefully mend the hole. Her kindness toward me was like sweet honey on a biscuit. I ate it up in one gulp. "Now put it on. I want to see how it looks." Anna did everything my mother didn't. She showed me how much she cared. How could I not adore her? I had never felt mother love like that.

———

Although Sotiris was my main boyfriend, my hormones were still raging. I loved kissing and petting with boys. With new freedom living at my father's place, I went out with Eddie and Alberto and anyone else who asked me. I also felt guilt and weakness of character. I should be loyal to Sotiris and stay home like a good Greek girl, patiently knitting until he came back from Korea? I didn't like staying home alone. I craved all the attention from the guys who gave it to me. Still my main interest was with Sotiris and my fantasy of happily ever after with him. After all, he was Greek, which automatically put a stamp of approval on him, where the other men in my life were Puerto Rican or Cuban.

I wrote Sotiris and I told him how much he meant to me, how I couldn't wait for his return, how I'd finally left and moved in with my father. I sent him gift packages. He encouraged my seeing his family and visits to New Jersey. He'd been gone almost a year.

When I learned he was coming home, I broke it off with the two other guys I was dating. All I wanted was Sotiris.

It was enchanting at first. We caught up with our lives. Together, we visited my mother and father in their separate places. We were serious. I was impatient to get going, to leave New York for California and start our new life together. I didn't believe it when Sotiris's true nature started to show. All I saw was how he was my ticket out of New York. I saw no other choices.

"When are you going to ask me to marry you?" I asked. "We need to make plans to go to California. Don't you want to start school?" He smiled. "Okay. Let's do it." We made it official by getting engaged.

To earn more money for my wedding gown and our trip west, I found part-time work at Alexander's Department Store in the lingerie department. I'd go there after I came home from my typing job at the bank. I liked my second job. He objected.

"Quit it," Sotiris said. "I don't like you working at night." I didn't want to quit. Another sign I ignored. He wanted all my time and attention, which I equated to love. His overbearing behavior bothered me, but I felt reluctant to confront him, or to create any discord between us. My need to leave New York overshadowed everything.

Miss Jackson had helped me handle problems with my mother. Now I told her about my boyfriend and shared my confused feelings. God, I wanted this guy to be the one. I loved Sotiris, yet I had doubts. "What shall I do?" I asked Miss Jackson. My body was in upheaval. Stomach cramps. Headaches. "You need to give this some thought," she said. "This is a major decision."

I didn't want to think. I wanted to leave New York. I couldn't see any other option. I had to say "I do" to Sotiris and suppress any doubts about our relationship.

We went ahead with plans to marry, setting a January date. My need to escape was overwhelming. Never mind the freezing New York weather. The sooner we left, the sooner Sotiris could start his education at the University of Southern California.

Even though I was living with my father at the time, I left for the wedding from my mother's apartment. She was pleased to see me carrying my wedding dress into her apartment. She helped me dress and zipped up the back of my gown. It surprised me to see her cry. Wasn't she glad to be rid of me? Instead she beamed and affectionately touched my face. A few of her Greek friends were there sipping coffee, nodding their approval. "Ah," one of the women said to me, "you look so beautiful." Now my mother showed pride, showing me off—the rebellious one, who shocked everyone and now was about to marry a decent Greek boy.

The wedding was a traditional Greek one. I went through it like a robot. My father walked me down the aisle. The service was long with many symbols, like *koufeta*—sugar almonds. Hardness for endurance of the marriage, sweetness for married life. The priest blessed the rings, the bride, and the groom three times. These rituals occurred throughout the service, to express the Holy Trinity. The crowns, the *stefana*, are the most important elements in the service. Two crowns, decorated with pearls, are placed on the bride and groom's head and exchanged three times. The *stefana* symbolize a long life together and are preserved in a special case and placed above the marital bed. My parents had one over theirs—so much for longevity in their marriage.

A week later, we packed the 1950 Buick convertible we'd bought to drive west. We scrounged money from the wedding gifts to get the car, and we set off for California.

From the first day, Sotiris and I disagreed and fought about everything. He wanted to buy things, souvenirs along the way. I wanted to protect our money for our life in California. He'd ask. "Do you have any money? I need some cigarettes."

We drove into California through Bakersfield. The weather was warm and sunny as we drove through rows of palm trees. Like a blind man seeing the sun for the first time,

I was ecstatic to see the tropical scenery. I buried my fears that I'd made a mistake. I had cut off my feelings while we were dating. Now I felt all of them. Before our marriage, I pretended to enjoy our intimacy. I acted like some two-bit actress doing anything to impress the director. Inside, I felt panicked. What had I done? Was it too late to turn back? Turn back to what? New York and to my parents?

———

In Los Angeles, we found a furnished apartment. I found yet another crummy typing job at an insurance company. Sotiris enrolled in the university.

From the start I could tell he was unhappy there. He complained about everything—his teachers, his classes, and his homework. What he really didn't like was getting up early for class and handing in homework. He stayed up late, watched TV, and missed classes. *Oh no*, I thought. *He's going to quit. There go my hopes and dreams.*

"I'm dropping out of school," he said halfway through the semester, and threw his textbook across the room.

I wanted to choke him. I wished him dead. If I'd had money, I'd have hired a Mafia hit man to do him in. Still, I clung to my illusion that with a little more effort on my part, this marriage could work. Like a mountain trekker with no guide for getting to the top, I just kept climbing.

I was determined to prove to my family that I was someone who had value and had married someone successful. How could I admit defeat? My Greek cultural training taught me to be the good submissive wife. I couldn't give up. Each wedding anniversary—first, second, third, fourth, and fifth—I'd ask myself, *Isn't it supposed to get better?* It didn't. I dreaded bedtime and his demands for sex. He smelled like a saloon at closing time, stinking of beer and cigarettes.

I could see no other way but for Sotiris to stay in school. If he dropped out, what kind of job could he get? Where would my fantasy go? I called his professors. "Please!" I begged. "Will you just tell him to stay?" They sympathized.

I had to face it. We were in our fifth year of marriage, and our shaky marriage was in shambles. I desperately searched for solutions.

There was a Greek church in Los Angeles. I called and prayed the priest would give me sage advice. I made an appointment to meet with him in his office, where icons of Christ and saints covered the walls. He was a tall, thin man with a gray beard. I kissed his hand in submission and deep respect. He wore a long black robe—typical attire for a priest. "Father, can you help me?" I begged.

I wept and told him my marriage was in crisis. Exhausted, I could not continue to send my husband through school. "He won't even get a job," I said. "What shall I do, Father? I don't want to leave and get a divorce. Please tell me what to do."

He stroked his beard deep in thought. We sat in silence for several minutes. I waited for his wisdom, his guidance. He'd tell me the right way to handle the problem. He looked at me.

"I can see you are a good wife and want to preserve your marriage. Here's what I think you need to do," he said, clearing his throat. He put his hands together in prayer. "The thing you should do is have a baby. A baby would solve your problems. With a child," he continued, "Sotiris is certain to get a job and become responsible. You will see him change. That's what you need to do." He got up, shook my hand, and walked me to the door. I was stunned. I sought spiritual guidance and got spiritual rubbish. What did he advise me to do? Get pregnant? A baby was the last thing I needed to save my marriage! This priest did not get it. If Sotiris couldn't be accountable toward me, his wife, I couldn't trust he'd be a responsible father either.

I called my family for support to see if anyone could help me deal with this dilemma. I hoped for some backing to leave this dying marriage. "He's okay," my sister said. "Just hang in there. Just go out with the guy and have some fun."

No one understood my anguish. I'd married someone cruel like my mother and irresponsible like my father. I'd created an even worse horror story than the one with my mother in New York. I was once more, in another prison with another warden. I hoped with time our relationship would improve; maybe I'd find a way to deal with Sotiris. But more anguish was about to come.

By 1960, we had been married for six years and I'd given up hope our life would get better. In fact, things got worse.

A neighbor with a litter of kittens gave us one. It was cuddly, soft, and adorable. I loved the kitten. I held it in my lap like a baby. I played with it. Perhaps my husband was jealous of the loving attention I gave the kitten. Sotiris was like a tyrant with the powerless animal. When the kitty had an accident, Sotiris smacked its bottom and forced its face in the pee. "Look what you did, bad cat." I had sympathy for the poor thing. We were alike. The helpless kitten could not escape; neither could I. He tortured both of us. If I hated Sotiris before, I now despised him.

Money was always an issue between us. Like my mother, I worried about the rent. I'd become just like her. How would I find money to pay it this month? We were always short.

One evening I sat waiting for Sotiris to come home. My husband burst into the apartment lugging a large new table lamp. I stood there in shock. "What the hell is that?" I asked when he smugly placed it on a table.

"Isn't it gorgeous?" he said proudly, as though he had found a hundred-dollar bill on the street. "It was on sale, and I had to buy it."

"Are you crazy?" I shook with rage. I wanted to kill him. I screamed, "We have no money for the rent, and you bought this lamp?" He ignored me and left the room. The rent check bounced that month, as usual.

A new neighbor, George, befriended my husband and introduced him to hunting and guns. Now Sotiris was fascinated with weapons and brought home a used rifle. I wondered if one of us, whoever grabbed it first, would shoot the other with it.

I thought I knew everything about Sotiris, but I was wrong. More shadow parts of him surfaced. He came home one evening with a small box.

"I bought a camera," he said, and unpacked the package. "I want to take some pictures of you." Pause. "In the nude."

I said, "No way." Why would he want to do that? He persisted.

"You have a beautiful body and I want to take photos of you." He convinced me they would be for his eyes only. We argued about it, but finally I gave in. He promised no one would see the photos.

A few weeks later I came home early from work and found the pictures of me in the nude lined up on the side of our bed. He'd been using my nude photos to masturbate. This man was more disturbed than I imagined. What else was he hiding from me?

"I want you to destroy those photos immediately," I said. "I'll rip them up right now if you don't." He looked down and was upset, not at what he'd been doing with the nude photos, but that he'd been caught. "Okay, okay," he said, averting my eyes.

Why didn't I leave then? Why didn't I pack my bags and get the hell out of that house and away from him? What kept me from leaving? The answer was complex.

One reason was my unbearable shame in facing my family with a failed marriage. If my parents could not sustain their relationship, well, I'd show them. I'd show my mother I could have a good marriage even though she didn't. No matter what happened, I'd hold mine together. I denied the reality of how bad it really was. Staying in my marriage reflected my low self-esteem, my disgrace in my failure to be a good, obedient, submissive wife.

In the Greek culture I was raised in, women had little value. From an early age, I believed I had no worth. Men were the important ones. I had this mistaken notion my husband could prove as an architect he was a talented somebody. Consequently, as his wife, I'd be somebody too. This strong, erroneous belief died hard.

The other reason I stayed was because of my in-laws. I'd done everything to convince them I'd be a virtuous wife to their son. I loved Anna, my sweet mother-in-law. How could I face her with my hatred for her son? He was her favorite. How could I admit my desperate need to leave him, but without losing her.

31. SHOPLIFTING

We sat in the dark of our Los Angeles apartment, eating leftover, cold pizza in the kitchen. Picking the cheese off the top of my pizza, I tried to swallow the lump in my throat. There had been no lights in the house for several days because we had no money to pay the electric bill. After too many years in this crumbling marriage, I felt an overwhelming urge to open the window and scream, "Help me, somebody!" to anyone passing in the street.

My husband, short and wide around the middle, gulped down a glass of wine poured from a peanut butter jar, wiping his red-stained mouth with his sleeve. The only sounds came from traffic outside with cars honking their horns and fire engines wailing their sirens, off to save some burning houses. *Hey,* I thought. *Why don't you guys come here, bring up your ladders, and save this crumbling marriage?*

The plan we'd agreed to was that I would work to support my husband's education to become an architect. My fantasy was my brilliant husband would design magnificent buildings for all to admire. I naively believed that he would complete his education with honors. We'd have lots of money from clients begging him to design their homes. Except Plan A was not working.

He told me he wanted to be an architect, to go to university. I believed him. But he had lied. Instead, he preferred to stay up late, a can of beer in one hand, cigarette in the other, his eyes glazed over, watching Steve Allen on the late show and skipping his classes the next day.

He yawned. "Maybe I'll look for a job tomorrow, pumping gas somewhere."

"Great idea," I'd said.

Look for a job? Who was he kidding? I knew he never would. I felt desperate, trapped in a dead-end marriage with no idea how to get out.

If I'd had any self-confidence, any voice to speak, I would have said, "Get off your fat, lazy ass and get any job. You pay for your own goddamn education! I'm through being your sugar momma, you piece of shit!" And then I'd pack a bag and get the hell out. But I didn't. I was a cowardly, submissive wife who kept silent and dutiful. That's what my mother had taught me. We are to serve and obey our husbands. Inside I seethed with bitter resentment.

All the fantasies I had about his becoming another Frank Lloyd Wright, designing unique, one-of-a-kind homes that everyone would want to visit, take pictures of, and hopefully duplicate, were like a Hollywood flick—a film noir.

Basically we had no extra money. We were in debt. My crappy job as a typist for an insurance company paid *bubkis*, as in barely enough to pay the rent and feed us, but not much more. My office was in downtown Los Angeles, within walking distance of the big department stores like Bullocks, Saks Fifth Avenue, and Macy's.

I spent my lunch hour browsing the various department stores, each one beckoning me to come in and buy something.

Every department had temptations to attract me: cosmetics, face creams, fragrances of perfume. I would dab Chanel on my neck and wrist, and try on the various shades of red lipstick, smearing them over my lips. Like a child in a candy store, I wanted to sample all the lotions, the face creams, the rainbow-colored eye shadow, the exotic-colored lipsticks—and I had no money to buy a thing.

Each day I would go to a different store, another department to browse, to sample, to touch something new. I would imagine if I could own that new fragrance to drive men crazy, wear that black slinky, tight-around-the-ass dress, it would transform me into a sexy movie star instead of the plain, lowly typist that I really was, wearing drab, threadbare dresses that looked like potato sacks on my small frame.

One day I was in the dress department of Bullocks looking at the dresses in my size. I took three of them into the fitting room to try them on. One of them was a dark blue-and-white slinky number with a plunging neckline. It fit tightly around my thighs and behind. *This dress looks good on me*, I said to myself. *I want it.* In that split second, I decided to take it, to wear it under my other dress, to just walk out of the store nonchalantly as though everything I had on belonged to me. At that moment there was no rational part of me that stepped back, looked at my behavior and said, *Hey. Stop right there. You're going to get caught. What the hell are you doing?* I just did it.

Walking out of the store with the new dress underneath my other dress that day was a thrill, a high. *It's mine*, I thought, *and I didn't get caught.* Like a drug user's first fix, the dress was like heroin rushing into my veins, giving me a feeling of euphoria. *Well*, I thought, *that was fun, but we can never do that again*—but I knew I was lying to myself.

If my deadbeat, lazy-assed husband would not get a job and buy me the things I wanted and felt I deserved, I was going to get them for myself. In my warped way of thinking, I felt the dress belonged to me, that I had every right to take it.

There was also a feeling of terror. I had taken pencils from a five-and-dime store as a child, but never anything as large as this. As I left the store with my heart beating like mad, I anticipated a tap on my shoulder from the security guard who would growl in my ear as he grabbed my arm, "Come with me, Miss. I know what you've got under your dress. You are under arrest."

When I took a lipstick or pair of earrings, I felt a thrill inside. Yet there was also a small part of me that knew if I continued to shoplift, eventually I'd get caught. Then I'd be punished severely not just for shoplifting, but for all the bad things I had ever done in my life.

I kept imagining the loud, booming voice of God. He was looking down from above, watching my every sinful act saying, "Someday I will punish you for what you are doing. You will pay. Just wait."

Each lunch hour was a new challenge, a new opportunity to take something I wanted and could never afford. The idea that I could get caught shoplifting did not prevent me from getting my daily fix. I was in great denial.

One day I went to the lingerie department, put on a black, lacy bra that gave my breasts an uplift, and wore it out of the store, leaving my old, out-of-shape one with the elastic all shriveled in the trash.

To try to save my marriage, I was seeing a new therapist who accepted my meager fee. He was in his sixties with bushy gray hair, deep blue eyes, and was heavy set. Better not to tell him about the stealing, of course, I rationalized. Much easier to talk about problems with my husband.

This therapist became a father figure. He'd put his hand on my shoulder as I left his office. "We'll work this out," he said. "Don't worry." I trusted his good judgment.

That's why I didn't want to tell him about the stealing. I knew what he would say. Even though I knew thieving was wrong, I didn't want to hear his admonishment, to stop my damaging behavior. Eventually after weeks of keeping it to myself, I couldn't hold onto the secret any longer, and told him everything about my shoplifting.

"I need those things I take," I told him. "My husband will never buy me those dresses, and the bras. He won't get a job. You know we're broke. How else would I get them?"

I braced myself for his response. The air was thick with his silence. He sat at his desk, tapping his pencil on the yellow tablet in front of him, perhaps hoping to tap some sanity into my self-destructive brain. He was not smiling. He cleared his throat, brought his wooden chair close to the couch where I sat with arms folded across my chest. He looked at me directly.

"Listen carefully to what I am about to say, because it's important. If you continue to shoplift, you will be caught and get arrested. I need you to know that if you go to jail, I will not go there and rescue you. I will not support what you are doing. Do you understand? You need to stop stealing right now." He let that sink in. I didn't like what he said, but I believed him.

I did not stop my criminal behavior right away. The last item I stole was a silk beige dress from Saks Fifth Avenue. I took it home. Except this time I did not intend to keep it. I let it sit there in my closet for a few days, needing to pretend for a little while longer it was mine.

A few days later, I knew what I had to do. I felt a great sadness as I took the dress out of the closet, touched and smelled the soft fabric. I put the dress in front of my body one last time. Under the kitchen sink, I found some brown wrapping paper and carefully packed the dress in it. With great reluctance to let the dress go, I wept. An old part of me that needed to leave was saying goodbye.

It broke my heart to let go of the dress as well as shoplifting. I slowly wrapped the piece of clothing, touching it tenderly, as though it were a beloved corpse. I carefully addressed the package to the store, carried it to the post office, and sent it back to where it belonged.

———

Tenaciously, I clung to the hope of finding a way to fix this broken relationship. Reality felt too unbearable to face. I returned to the therapist in L.A., who I saw as a father figure. I hoped he would give me better advice than the priest. "Please," I begged. "Can you tell me what to do to save my marriage? Just don't tell me to divorce him," I said. "I can't do that." I knew my family would blame me and say it was my fault. Instead of showing pride (look at my wonderful marriage), I'd be humiliated.

Week after week, over and over, I begged the therapist for answers. He wouldn't do it.

"I can't tell you what to do," he said. Then one day he paused and leaned forward. "But I'd like to offer a suggestion." *At last*, I thought. *Something I should contemplate.* "Don't think of a divorce," he said. "What you might consider is a temporary separation. You both could take a break, date others to help you decide whether you want to reconcile or sever ties." What a brilliant idea.

The revelation that followed soon thereafter was that my crumbling marriage was over. The reality I denied with shoplifting was that my husband was not about to change no matter what I did. He would never attend classes, get good grades, finish college, or become an architect. He would never get a job, pay the bills, or give me a decent allowance.

He was never going to buy me all the beautiful clothes I wanted. That fantasy was over.

My husband would never allow me to leave if he were at home. He'd block the door and bolt it. I planned a time when Sotiris was away. I stuffed some clothes in a shopping bag and ran out the door. At the click of the door, I felt like I'd left my jail cell for good. The click was just like the one I'd heard when I left my mother's apartment. I flew down the stairs.

The rooming house I found had a small space in an attic with a cot and a dresser. I was in ecstasy. For me the room was more than a refuge. It was a palace, my very own castle.

Sotiris went crazy. He called me at the office. "Baby, baby," he begged, "I'll get a job. I promise to pay the bills. I'll go to therapy. I'll do anything. Just don't leave me. Come back."

But it was too late. After eating bitter poison on a daily basis, freedom tasted like a chocolate truffle, sweet and delicious. I could never return. My temporary separation was bliss. I'd never felt such liberty to explore the world around me.

I dated like crazy, as if I'd never been out before. Whenever any man took me to dinner, I went to bed with him out of gratitude. Wasn't that what I was supposed to do? How do other women behave? I asked my therapist. My appreciation for men's attention knew no bounds. Isn't sex part of a date? "What's normal?" I asked.

"You don't even owe your date a kiss goodnight," he said. Unbelievable. "You are more than just your body. You have a brain. Use it." A brain? Who, me?

I found strength from the therapist and, shaking with fear, divorced Sotiris. At last. Freedom. Like the friends who saw my mother as a kind old lady, my friends saw Sotiris as a nice guy. They'd say, "I saw him at a downtown café, and he said he still loves you. He wants you back. Maybe you two could reconcile?" Not in a million, trillion years.

Friends continued to run into Sotiris. They'd see him at someone's dinner party. He'd say the same thing, that he still loved me and wanted me back.

He'd call me from time to time with different excuses. "I just made your favorite Greek soup," he'd say. "How about coming over?" Or, "My mother is visiting from New York. Wouldn't you like to come over and see her?" I knew these were pretexts to put me back in his grip and control me. I'd thank him and decline. I was afraid if I did see him again he'd find a way to entice me back into that dark cave of hell. I went ahead with the divorce.

32. SYNANON FIX

Months passed. I was lonely and wanted to meet new friends. No, I wanted to meet new men. I wanted someone who would give me a new direction I needed. My marriage had confined me to a prison-like existence. My husband had dominated every aspect of my life: what to wear, who to talk with, what classes I should take. At twenty-seven, this ladybird was ready to spread her new wings.

A girlfriend mentioned an interesting place on the beach in Santa Monica where addicts went to recover. Everyone talked about this new hot spot. Even *Life* magazine devoted a full issue to Synanon. My friend said, "There are cute guys there, I hear."

"Really? What else?" I asked.

"They have open house every Saturday night. There's a discussion around a topic. Everyone there kicks it around. Later there's live music and dance. We get to meet new guys. Doesn't it sound like fun? Let's check it out."

This "in" place intrigued me. My dark fascination involved meeting tall, handsome, and dangerous men. I wanted to hear how they recovered from their painful addictions. What would these guys look like? How would they act? I'd always had interest in what made people change. Maybe I could learn something from them to make some changes in my unstable life.

"Yes," I said. "Let's go there." I wanted to see this place. It beat blind dates and hanging out in bars to meet men. The whole scene sounded exciting and a little scary. I thought it would be safe to go to an open house.

The following Saturday, we dolled up and went to see what all the fuss was about. The Synanon house stood right on the beach in Santa Monica. The building was huge with many rooms. The setting with sounds of ocean waves surrounding it aroused the romantic part of me.

The place was packed with people when my friend and I entered. At the door, a drop-dead gorgeous guy greeted me. His movie-star looks, tall with thick brown hair to his shoulders and deep blue eyes, enchanted me. I caught a whiff of musk. He wore a tan sports jacket and a white shirt with neat jeans. Clean cut. My friend was right. They did have good-looking guys here. He took my hand and with a smile said, "Welcome to Synanon. Please go in and find a seat." *Oh my*, I thought. *This is really nice. Lead me on.*

The meeting had already started when I squeezed into my seat. I saw a topic written on a blackboard in front of their dining hall—some quote from a philosopher, an author, something provocative to stimulate discussion. I didn't want to participate. I just wanted to see what happened, to check things out. I sat there enthralled. These men were not just attractive; they were intelligent as well, which impressed me. *Maybe*, I thought, *there's someone I'd meet who was right for me.* It was electrifying to be there. Even the air in the place sizzled.

Afterwards we all socialized. The musicians brought their instruments to the stage and entertained the guests. Joe

Pass, a celebrity resident, played guitar. On the outside, he'd accompanied Ella Fitzgerald in concerts. The place crackled with excitement, and I knew I was in the middle of a lot of dynamic energy.

On my first visit I mingled with the residents. Everyone I spoke with was friendly, welcoming. They were openhearted people. My self-esteem, never strong, had fallen into a dark hole following my divorce. It meant a lot to have men approach and show interest in me. Each week I eagerly went back.

The men were genuinely attentive. "Who are you?" they'd ask. "How are things going?" And they shared their life stories too; we had a lot in common with our abusive childhoods and poverty. I felt a closeness to everyone I spoke with. Like a well-worn shoe, Synanon felt comfortable. I couldn't wait to go back.

They asked about my work, where I came from, my interests. We even talked about my recent divorce. They sympathized and understood how bad I felt. These openhearted people liked and accepted me. "Come back," they said. And I did. Every time I walked in the place, I got smiles of welcome. For months thereafter I returned every Saturday night. I was hooked.

Synanon became my new family. I had none in New York, and with my husband gone, I had none in Los Angeles either. I'd found my new home.

I would learn eventually that my addiction was a bit different from theirs. Mine was to the idea that I could find a family that would accept me. What I didn't realize was the high price I'd have to pay. My ultimate goal in life was to find a home where I belonged. I thought I'd found it. I believed I'd found a place that included and wanted me in it. Synanon, my fantasy fix.

Over the following months I became more absorbed in family life there. I helped sort the laundry, fixed sandwiches, and looked for other ways to volunteer. Women residents and their children had satellite housing. They needed someone to babysit the children when the women went to meetings at the main house. I signed up eagerly and read and played with the children. I took them on outings to parks and museums. I didn't just put my toe in the water—I dove in.

But soon something critical happened to create a shocking new view of my fantasy home.

An important aspect of Synanon was focused on the "Synanon Game." Members met in groups. If someone was screwing up, they aimed their attention on him. They didn't let anyone get away with bullshit. They'd pounce on him, and cut him down. With no holds barred, they'd let him have it. "You fucked up!" they'd say. The purpose was to force the person to look at himself, how he messed up, face it, and change his behavior. These verbal attacks were called "haircuts." The two rules in the Game were no physical violence and no leaving the group. But there was a lot of verbal brutality. Your ass stayed in the seat until the session was over.

The Game intrigued me. We outsiders in the community wanted to get involved in it too. We wanted to experience change in our lives as well. I know I did. When groups were formed for people in the community, I eagerly joined one. Now I was really ready to jump in and participate.

I wanted everyone in Synanon to like me. I'd try to impress them with how delightful and generous I was. I wanted to show them only my good side: the part of me that was accepting, eager to please and participate. I concealed the other part: the one full of fear, the one full of yearning to belong and be a part of their family. They saw right through my facade. They'd nail me every time.

"Why don't you cut your ain't-I-sweet bullshit," someone in the group would say. "When the hell are you going to get real?" I couldn't get away with anything. I'd get a haircut.

I was ill-prepared for these clashes. Yet I'd go back for more. I'd be confronted by everyone in the group who saw through my goody-two-shoes front. In these attacks they'd cut off more than my ego. I'd drive home in tears. I needed them to see me as someone wonderful and special. I wanted everyone to accept me, defects and all. Isn't that what good families did? These people were significant in my life. They were family. I wanted their approval. What I didn't see was their cruelty covered by so-called good intentions. I was replicating the same abuse I'd had in my marriage and in the family I left in New York.

I'd had little experience being single. I'd gone from home to marriage. Now I dated anyone who asked me out. With Synanon my new home, my date and I would hang out there. The residents became like the brothers I always wanted. And I was their kid sister. My real brother hardly spoke to me. We'd never been close. The men at the house would check out the guys I brought over and give their frank opinion about them.

"He's not bad, but pretty square," they'd say about one. "What do you see in this guy?" they'd ask me about another. I hung on their every word.

The men who had seniority and had been in recovery for a year had more freedom. I dated a few. I felt flattered to be invited out to a movie with one of them, but I knew everything that happened between us would be reported and scrutinized. Even without a chaperone, I felt an invisible Synanon spirit observing us on our dates.

Then one Saturday night after a dinner date which included several glasses of wine, I suggested a visit to Synanon. At the entrance, one of the head honchos took me aside. He looked me in the eye and said, "I can tell you've been drinking. I can't let you come in." He stood at the door blocking my entry. "You need to leave now. Don't come back here like that."

I felt stripped bare, exposed, and ashamed. I left. My date tried to console me, but I knew he didn't get it.

"You didn't drink that much," he said. "What's their problem anyhow?"

Was I pushing the boundaries of what was acceptable? It never even occurred to me that it was inappropriate to go to a place where residents were recovering from addictions and just waltz in with wine on my breath. I dreaded my next visit.

I knew they would nail me at the next group meeting. I was braced to get the Synanon-style haircut. When I walked in, no one spoke to me. Everyone at the house knew what had happened. Now they were going to let me have it. I sat down with the group surrounding me with looks of contempt.

"What the hell are you doing here anyhow?" one of the guys challenged me. "You act like you can just come here with all your boyfriends and not contribute a dime to this place. You show no respect for us when you've been out on a date and then waltz your big ass in here, half-drunk, and expect us to welcome you. Who the fuck do you think you are?" I cried, but there was no letup.

"Yeah. Yeah. Just boo-hoo all you want. You're just pathetic. You're a fucking phony. We don't want you here, anymore, get it?" A one-two punch and I was out for the count.

No matter what I said to defend myself, they turned away. I told them I was sorry. And I'd only had two drinks. I told them I'd never do it again. No matter what I said, they turned away. Their words stung me. I didn't want their judgment. I wanted their forgiveness.

I no longer felt welcomed at Synanon. I'd hit bottom.

I avoided facing my insensitivity to these people in their vulnerable state. I couldn't see that being around recovering addicts with alcohol on my breath was unacceptable, even detrimental to their recovery. I was blind to their needs.

Finally, I got it. Okay. I felt I'd acted like an immature kid, seeking an idealized family, one that would give me unconditional acceptance. Did I deserve their haircut? It might have been too harsh for my Synanon offense, yet the experience felt like one of my mother's beatings. No, they didn't physically strike me as she had, but their words stung like a whipping nonetheless. As a rebellious teen, I felt I deserved my mother's attacks. But I didn't need pain any more. And I had to face a tough reality: they were not my family.

I also realized that Synanon pushed me to see some unacceptable things about myself. Not a pleasant experience, but I don't know where else I would have learned these things.

I stayed away from Synanon for several weeks. I needed some perspective on the whole situation. I had some thinking to do. I could see I had an unpaid debt. Apparently being a volunteer was not enough. I needed to give them something more, like money. I sat down and wrote a check and sent it to Synanon. I received a personal thank you response from Chuck Dederich—the head man at Synanon. He urged me to return.

"We miss you. You are always welcome here," the note said. The big chief acknowledged me. I held on to the letter for a long while. I treasured the words he wrote. I felt I was getting approval from a father figure. At the time, I still needed that. A few weeks later I threw the note away. I no longer needed their validation. Something in me had changed. I still yearned for the loving, all-accepting family. But I already had a family. Not a perfect one, nonetheless it was mine. But for now, I realized my time with Synanon was over. I was done.

33. SEARCHING FOR
MY FATHER IN ATHENS

My travel plans for Europe in the 1960s did not include a visit to Greece. I was in my thirties and wanted to see Europe. My father had taken a trip to visit his brother in the late 1950s with his second wife Fanny, an American. He liked the easy life there so much he decided to retire there. Fanny didn't like Greece at all and returned to New York. She hoped my father would miss her and leave Greece. Instead my father divorced her.

I had no intention of visiting him. I had only anger for this man. I blamed him for leaving my illiterate mother with no financial resources. He'd dumped my mother, married wife number two, and moved to Athens. When wife number two left Greece, the matchmakers found him his third wife, a spinster. He hadn't changed his womanizing ways. I had no interest in seeing my father ever again.

A stop to visit an uncle in France changed my mind about Greece. Uncle George looked like a big stuffed teddy bear, a bushy beard—all warm and cuddly. We sat at his wooden kitchen table after a dinner of lamb stew with a lot of red wine. I confided in him, told him I was estranged from the entire family, including my father. I was adamant. No intention to visit Greece.

"Listen to me, my child," Uncle George said, drinking his cognac and speaking to me like a father. "You must go to Greece and see the village where your mother came from. You have aunts and cousins living there." He stroked his beard thoughtfully and filled his glass once again. "Family is very important," he said firmly. "I know all the relatives would want to meet you." He took my hand. "You have an opportunity now, and you must go to Greece."

I changed my plans and booked passage to Athens. I had carried my father's address with me in case I changed my mind. When I landed in Italy, I wrote a hasty postcard to him. I told him I'd be in Greece soon and maybe we could meet.

The plane was delayed. Instead of eleven at night, it arrived at three in the morning. The airport was deserted. I wondered if my father had been there to meet my plane at all or if maybe he was angry with me and had decided not to show. The bus took us to the center of Athens. At one of the all-night taverns I spoke to a man who directed me to a cheap place to stay. I felt I'd easily locate my father the following day. It turned out to be not as easy as I imagined.

Sure I was angry at my father for his irresponsibility, yet a big part of me still wanted to see him again, to deal with unresolved issues from the past. What would he look like? Had he changed? Could we make up?

The August morning was hot and muggy in my small room. I hurried out of the hotel to find a phone to call my father. I approached a policeman and explained the situation. He pointed out a phone booth, the telephone directory, and explained how to use tokens. My father's name, Costa Fotopulos, was as common as John Smith in the States. I groaned.

A woman answered the first call. *"Embros"* (Hello), she said. I tried to act confident but I felt shy and stammered, "My name is Irene and I'm searching for my father, Costa. Is your husband from America?"

"Oh no, dear," she replied sadly. "He's from Crete." Each call I made was a futile act. Why had I come to Greece? I went through all the C's under Fotopulos with no luck. I had my father's address and could just call a cab to take me there. I'd already been rejected by him. He had left me. What if my letter had pissed him off, and he hadn't even shown up at the airport? No, better not take that chance.

Yet now that I was in Athens, I didn't want to give up on finding him. I had unfinished business with him, and I had a need to face him about past issues.

Then I remembered my father had a brother, Theodore. Maybe a call to him would bring me closer to reaching my father. It was still early in the day, yet my armpits were drenched in sweat. I bought more telephone tokens.

There were four Theodores in the book. By now I had the speech down pat, about where I was from and how I was searching for my father. Some of the women I spoke with were so eager to help me that, even though their husbands were not related, they'd almost invite me over for dinner. That's how the Greeks are—very hospitable.

It was the fourth Theodore in the book and I had started the usual, "Does your husband have a brother named Costa?"

I could hear excitement in her voice. "Yes, yes. He does. And I am your Aunt Chrissa. *Kalos eirthes*" (Welcome), she said. Bingo, the right number at last.

"I'm not sure my father wants to see me," I said. "I wrote him a letter a few months ago." She wouldn't let me finish. Greeks love drama, the crazier the better.

"You mustn't worry about a thing," she said happily.

"We'll take care of everything." My cousins Mimi and Photis would pick me up from the hotel. "Pack up," she said. "We all want to meet you." She said she'd contact my father and have him meet me at her home. I'd never met my aunt, yet I felt I'd known her all of my life.

The cousins, two tall, gorgeous, young men arrived at my hotel an hour later and whisked me away to their house on the outskirts of Athens. When the cab stopped, my father was at the door to greet me.

Time stopped. There he stood. I'd found my father at last. We cried and held each other. I could smell some aftershave on his smooth-skinned face. He looked the same, not much different than five years earlier. A little more gray in his full head of hair. Still captivating with his warm eyes. He always dressed well and wore a white sport shirt along with beige linen slacks. This was my father, and I loved him all over again.

My aunt had all my favorite foods—moussaka, pastitsio, black kalamata olives, a big green salad with thick slices of feta cheese. There were bottles of ouzo and retsina, a nasty-tasting wine. We talked about the New York family and my trip to Greece. We made plans to go to town the next day and have breakfast together.

Over coffee and *loukoumathes* (Greek doughnuts), I told my father why I hadn't planned to come to Greece. I told him I was angry that he left me, how I never knew how to find him because he moved so often. "I needed you Pop." I told him I had wanted his protection from my mother's rages and beatings.

"That woman was crazy," he said. "Why do you think I left her so many times?" Then came all the bullshit lies, how he tried to contact me many times, but my mother's threats to send him to jail, to kill him and his girlfriends, and other accusations put him off. So he retreated. I wasn't buying it. I had many more questions. Why didn't he try harder to reach us? Why didn't he pay child support? Why did he run from us? He sat there in silence chain-smoking his Greek cigarettes.

I knew there were things he'd never be able to explain. I would have to accept this was my father. Not easy. I still wanted answers. There was nothing I could do to change this man. I knew that, in spite of his faults, I still loved him.

He asked about my job. Was I making good money? I think he hoped I'd give him some. He hadn't changed; he was still self-centered. He seemed surprised I worked and went to college at night.

"How did you do all that on your own?"

I told him it wasn't easy. I worked hard. Money was scarce.

He slipped me a few drachmas when I left, a small gesture to erase his guilt for not paying for my education. I felt a mixture of sadness and resignation. My stomach hurt.

"You know what?" I said, folding my hands together. "There are some conversations between us which will always remain unfinished."

We sat there in silence at the café. People walked past us. Cars honked. I could see my father was uncomfortable with beads of sweat on his face. Even though it was only ten in the morning, my father pushed his coffee aside. He called the waiter over and ordered a double shot of ouzo.

————

After I left for California, I continued contact with my father by phone and made additional visits to Greece. We had established a new relationship, and I wanted to build on it. In truth, I gave him an opportunity to right the wrongs between us. I wanted him to make up for all the years we were apart and lavish me with praise for my perseverance to get an education on my own. Could he see me and what I'd accomplished on my own? I wanted so much from him that I'd missed. The child in me wanted my father back.

Whenever I arrived in Greece, I felt good to see him at first. But we'd always end up fighting over the same old issues. Why did he leave? Why didn't he stay in touch? Why didn't he send financial support? I wanted him to write a big check for my mother and give it to me. As if there were an amount big enough to make up for the times she had to scrape by on so little.

"Please tell your mother I'm sorry," I wanted him to say. "I wasn't a very good husband." For myself, I wanted an apology from him for going off on his own, never letting us know how to reach him. I wanted him to know I wanted his protection from my mother's beatings. I really wanted him to know how much we all missed him. How much we loved and needed him.

I softened toward him in the end. His own father had died when he was two. His mother married a cruel stepfather who mistreated and sent him away. I realized my father couldn't parent me when he'd had no role models of his own. Yet he would still remain my father.

34. SAM

After another breakup with the latest fling, I decided to attend a group therapy retreat in Los Angeles. That's where I met Sam, an engineer. He looked to be in his forties like me, and had those rugged good looks that physically attracted me just like those ads with a cowboy on a fence, a Marlboro cigarette dangling from his mouth. We sat together at dinner and talked. He was from New York too. I felt a familiar easy feeling being with him, like with a broken-in shoe. There was a magnetic physical attraction between us. Between group sessions, we took walks together and one night just after he walked me to my cabin door, he kissed me. I wanted to see him again after the retreat. I was in heat to have an affair with Sam. Except there was a small problem.

He was married. He told me it was an unhappy relationship. His wife was bipolar. He said he had two children—a daughter, ten, and a son, six.

This was not what I signed up for. I wanted a man that was free, unencumbered, without any complicated ties. A single man, and ready to settle down—that's what I wanted.

That wasn't Sam. He had a lot of baggage I wasn't ready to deal with. Yet, I wanted to see him again. I didn't want to let him go.

After the retreat we found ways to meet. It was exciting sex with Sam, which drew me closer to him. I wanted more time with him. But, at some point, I knew it would be futile to continue this affair. He didn't love his wife but he was a devoted father. I had to face that this thing we had would not be right for either of us. I tried to break it off.

"Listen," I said to him. "I can't do this anymore. We have to break up. I hate when you leave me. I want to be with you all the time. It's not going to work. Let's just end it." He looked at me.

"Who said this was going to be easy?" he said. "I don't want you to leave." He put his arms around me. "I love you. Don't give up on us. We'll work it out." I gave in.

A few weeks later Sam came to my apartment and looked upset. "What's wrong?" I asked.

"Make me a drink," he said. "A stiff one. I told my wife I'm leaving her."

I was both happy and concerned. What would our new relationship look like after his separation? He looked shattered but determined to go through with his planned split.

Sam found a small apartment in downtown L.A. and started divorce proceedings, which were ugly and endless with child support issues, alimony, and things I didn't want to hear about. I wanted romance with Sam not drama.

Where I enjoyed a glass of wine on weekends, I noticed Sam drank several glasses every night. I excused his drinking as a way for him to deal with his separation from his children and the pending divorce. With sympathy I even bought his liquor. *Poor guy,* I thought. *Of course he needs a few drinks to deal with this difficult situation.*

The children were a problem for me because I had none and knew nothing about parenting a ten-year-old girl and six-year-old boy. I felt guilt that I'd taken their father away from them.

We argued. I wanted Sam to myself and didn't know how to handle my feelings. Intellectually, I believed the children should spend time with their father. But emotionally, like a child with a new toy, I didn't want to share him. I was just like the fairytale: a wicked, selfish stepmother.

When Sam's divorce came through, I pressed for marriage. He resisted. "What's the hurry?" he asked. The hurry for me was I was ready to settle down, have a home, and with my biological clock ticking, have some children.

When I was admitted to a Sacramento university to get my master's degree, he followed me there. "I don't want to lose you," he said.

In new surroundings, we sought therapy to help us struggle with the issue of our relationship and marriage. Were we going forward? When I threatened to end it once again, he relented, and we made plans to wed.

We had a small marriage ceremony with a few close friends to help us celebrate. I was pleased to seal our relationship. I thought marriage to Sam would solve all our problems. I loved and believed in him.

What I've learned with great pain and sorrow is when you meet a man with potential, untapped possibilities, run, do not walk, to the nearest exit. Correction: do not run, *fly* to the nearest exit. I had a problem choosing men who had brains but no ambition or purpose to achieve their potential.

My hope was that Sam would leave his career as an engineer, complete his college degree, and ideally I saw us as two bright therapists working together. I was happy when he registered at the local university. But some ghost from the past reared its ugly head.

Sam had problems with a teacher he didn't like. He was a tough professor who required his students to write challenging papers. Sam balked and decided to drop out of the class and school. I urged him not to. "Hang in there," I said, and eagerly wrote his assignments for him. When I got tired and suggested he write his own papers, he did drop out. In retrospect, there was a familiar pattern about Sam's drama. Let's pause here. Didn't my ex-husband also have great potential and drop out of school? How did I miss their similarities?

Sam's drinking increased. We fought over his children, visitations, and his crazy ex-wife. On and on it went. The physical intimacy we enjoyed early in our relationship diminished.

Unexpectedly the engineering company he worked for offered Sam a two-year contract to work in South America. Would I go with him? "Of course not," I said. How could I just drop everything as a graduate student when I was in the middle of writing my dissertation?

"Couldn't you finish it later?" he asked. Sam was angry I would not drop out of school to join him. He threatened divorce. I loved this man but didn't want to interrupt my education and go anywhere. I suggested we find good counsel to help us, and Sam agreed to go to couples therapy to resolve the issue.

The couples therapist we saw listened patiently to us both. He respected Sam's determination to leave and work in South America and understood my need to stay and complete my education. We had long sessions together. He saw us two, sometimes three, times a week before Sam was to leave for his assignment. He became our wise advisor.

In our last session together, he proposed it was right for Sam to go to South America and it was best for me to stay in school and finish my degree. He urged me to build a bridge of connection between us and visit Sam during the school holidays. I agreed and hoped we could salvage our shaky relationship. I counted the days until I could get my degree and join Sam in South America. I loved this man and was willing to do what I could to make our marriage work. We agreed that while we were apart we might have affairs, but ultimately, we would place our relationship first.

My visits to South America during school holidays were like mini-honeymoons. We'd plan excursions to museums and neighboring towns, savor Spanish wines with delicious paella, and enjoyed exciting intimacy in bed. I had renewed hope for our marriage.

After graduation I eagerly joined Sam with hopes of having big festivities, rekindling our relationship, and even starting a family. How could I foresee the horror that lay ahead?

Instead of a great reunion and celebration with Sam, what happened next was shocking and devastating.

When we met at the airport, I saw a grieving man. Sam had lost weight and had aged since I last saw him. He had dark circles under his eyes as though he hadn't slept for many nights. His clothes hung on him like he'd slept in them, all crumpled and wrinkled. A man who previously had impeccable hygiene now smelled as though he hadn't bathed for days. Who was this stranger that resembled my husband? What happened to the man I once knew and loved?

Sam confessed to an affair gone tragic. He became involved with a woman at his company who fell in love with him and wanted to marry him. She asked Sam to divorce me. When he refused, she cut her wrists and committed suicide.

He was inconsolable, despairing, a grief-stricken man. For me it was a breaking point. I was unable to forgive, comfort Sam, or try to fix our broken marriage.

I realized it was over between us before Sam's South American work assignment was completed. When we returned home, it became official. Our marriage was now over.

35. JUST KISS ME
ONE MORE TIME

After my divorce from Sam, I felt like a total failure at marriage and all relationships. One divorce was bad, but two were too much. I questioned what went wrong: how did I flop again? But I gave up seeking answers. After Sam had been gone for several months, I was 47 now, lonely and deserted. I thought of meeting new men, but who would want someone like me who flunked Relationship 101?

On a walk I spotted a flyer on a College Avenue light post which read "Tired of the bar scene and want to make new friends? New in the community and want to meet new friends? We're a group of men and women who meet monthly to discuss books, movies, and plays. Bring a dish to share and come join us." The address was on Telegraph Avenue in Berkeley.

A community of interesting people discussing books and theater felt much better than the bar scene. I tried that. I'd go in to some dive, find a stool, and order a glass of house white wine. I hoped to meet some nice-looking guy, lonely like me, both of us seeking someone special, someone to take inner pain away. Instead I'd end up with a one-night stand and a bad hangover the next day. What the hell was I doing to myself? Enough. Time to try something different.

I went through my closet and found some slacks that fit and a colorful shirt. We can do it, I said to myself. I can always leave if it feels too uncomfortable.

The flyer was taped on the door of the Department of Labor and Mental Health building. The title of the building made me wonder what lay beyond the door. I felt a knot in my stomach. Deep breath first. Okay. Let's do it. I opened the door.

About twenty men and women of all ages occupied the room, talking together, milling about with plates of food and glasses of wine in their hands. I felt uncomfortable, a misfit. I felt old, unattractive, and unappealing. Maybe I had made a mistake to venture out.

Then I recognized a woman from my neighborhood. Several people stood around her talking. She waved to me and patted the seat next to hers.

"Come over here," she said, "I want you to meet someone." She pointed to an attractive man standing next to her. "This is John. He's new to the area."

What I noticed first were his deep, blue eyes, and then his wavy, blond hair all the way down to his shoulders. He was tall, about six feet, and slender. He wore casual clothes, neat blue jeans, and a white T-shirt with Berkeley on it. He smiled and said, "Hi." Drop-dead gorgeous. He looked at me with interest.

"So what kind of work do you do?" John asked.

I couldn't get over his good looks. My tongue stuck to the roof of my mouth. I knew if I spoke any words they would make no sense at all. My guess was he modeled for some men's sports magazine.

"I work for a labor union," he offered.

"I'm a psychologist," I murmured.

"We're in the right place." He laughed circling his hand in the air, motioning to the whole building. "Me in labor, you in mental health." He looked at the buffet table. "I'm hungry," he said. "What did you bring?"

We walked over to the feast of food with bowls of salads and other dishes. He looked at the gourmet selections. I showed him my vegetable with pasta casserole. He got a plate and filled it.

"Hmm," he said swallowing a bite. "You made this? Tastes good. What's in it?"

We discussed the ingredients of my offering, a broccoli-pasta-mushroom casserole. John polished off the entree, wiped his mouth on his sleeve, and heaped more of my dish on his plate. I loved men with good appetites.

We exchanged telephone numbers. I thought he was being polite. Probably collected women's phone numbers and tossed them in the trash at the end of the evening. Would he save mine? Then someone came into the center of the room and clapped his hands for attention.

"Okay," the man said. "Time to break up into groups and discuss the book. Let's reconvene in an hour."

There was a small space in the room for six of us to gather and discuss the topic. John turned and went into the next room to join another group. I wondered if I'd see him later.

Our gathering enjoyed lively conversation. The book was Herb Goldberg's *The Hazards of Being Male*. Many found it controversial. I got caught up in everyone's opinion on the subject. Hazards? I never saw hazards for any male in my Greek culture.

Afterwards we all went back to the living room to have a broader discussion with a leader moderating the topic. These bright, Berkeley types had strong opinions on the subject of men and their roles in the family and work place. I had never questioned the role of the male in my Greek society. Mostly I just listened.

Later we socialized around a dessert table full of cookies, cakes, and brownies. John was talking with a young woman. She was tall and slender with blond long hair. This stunning young lady looked at John adoringly.

"Hey," she said, "why don't you come over sometime this week? I'm back from a trip to Europe and I have some slides I want to show you."

I bet she also had other things she planned to show him too. What was left of my low self-esteem plummeted to zero. I grabbed my jacket and slunk out the door. Well, there went another possibility. I'd never see that guy again.

That week had me studying for the psychology licensing exam—again. By Friday I was spent, sick of every single textbook—abnormal psychology, child psychology, forensic psychology. Yuck. No more of that. A break was what I needed. I dug into my purse to find John's telephone number. Maybe I'd invite him over for wine and cheese. When I reached for the phone, I saw I had a message.

"Hi," he said. "This is John. How about having dinner with me tomorrow?"

Would I? Of course I would. I called him back and invited him over for dinner to sample my signature dish: Greek chicken. Drench a chicken with lemon and white wine. Sprinkle the bird with butter, salt, pepper, rosemary, and oregano. Bake two hours at 350 degrees—voila. Perfect and tasty every time. I hoped he'd like it and take second helpings.

John came over the next night. The first thing he did was greet me with a hug. Then he spotted my cat Zorba. Uh-oh. Zorba didn't like anybody. That feline usually hid under the couch when strangers came to visit. Still John went over and picked him up. Zorba just purred and rubbed his face against John's. My cat never purred like that in my arms. You'd think those two guys had been buddies for years. I stood there watching this event. Was this guy a charmer with everybody? If my cat Zorba gave his approval, this man had just overcome an important barrier to my house and my heart.

After dinner with second helpings from my chicken dish, John put his feet up on the couch and cuddled my cat. I put some jazz music on the stereo. This guy knew how to make himself comfortable. I liked that. I felt immense gratitude that this sweet, appealing man would share a dinner with me. I didn't believe I could attract a toad, let alone a prince. We both felt comfortable to talk about our lives.

He told me he'd broken up with someone recently. He'd been in a long-term relationship with a woman who had four children. She wanted a further commitment and he didn't. I wanted to know more details but instead shared I'd just ended a ten-year marriage with two stepchildren.

I thought of the young woman at the discussion group. He was probably going to see her again and five other women he'd met that night. This was nothing serious. I could see this would be a casual friendship and that's what I wanted too. Good. A farewell hug at the door and he was gone. No problem. I was fine with that.

John called a week later and asked me out. I was surprised. I hadn't dated in years and didn't know what the rules were. How to dress, how to speak, how to act—all this was brand new to me. I'd forgotten how to behave with someone on a date.

"What am I supposed to do?" I asked my new therapist. "How do people do dating? Why is this guy calling me?" My insides were twisted into a pretzel.

"Relax," she said. "Just be yourself."

Not what I wanted to hear. I needed a map. I wanted directions.

Next John invited me to visit his apartment. There was scarcely anything in it. He had no television, just lots of books and many jazz and classical records. The worn couch was stuffed in the corner of the living room. A wooden table and two chairs filled his small kitchen. Sparse. This was such a nice guy, full of positive energy. Yet the world he lived in looked so monastic. John intrigued me.

We continued to date—dinners, attending movies, with outings to the city and a local Berkeley flea market. I still couldn't believe this appealing man was interested in going out with me. Something I was doing was charming this guy. If we were playing a board game like Clue, I'd roll the dice and know who did it, the weapon used, and in what room they committed the murder. This was a different game I had no idea how to play.

Then there was—uh-oh—the fact that I was falling in love with this guy. That was scary beyond belief. This couldn't last. I knew he'd eventually leave me and that our affair would end in disaster. I'd had crushes and affairs before. They all started out hopeful with a lot of passion, and then ended in ruin. I didn't want that familiar great pain of loss again. I already felt like a reject, and fear had become a regular part of me. Still we continued to meet.

———

He invited me to go camping with him in the Sierras. I was a city girl, not a camper, but I went. John introduced me to the infinite world of nature and wildlife. He showed me how to pitch a tent and how to zip our sleeping bags together. At night, he'd build a fire. We'd sit close on a bench, open some wine, and listen to the sounds of nature around us. He'd grill some sausages and vegetables while I prepared a salad. After dinner we'd walk around the campgrounds and look up at the sky. I'd never seen so many stars like that before. Everything was strange and new with this guy.

In the morning we'd hike through the forest. He introduced me to his fascination with trees. We looked at the ones around us and explored the many varieties. This man was like someone from another galaxy, like no one I'd been with before. He had a wide-eyed way of viewing the world and it was all so enchanting to me.

I'd been with many men before, but I never felt such love for a guy as I did with John. Still I kept pushing him away, telling him to leave, go away. We needed to end it. What else could I do but prepare myself for his departure? When he said he loved me. I couldn't believe it.

"This is not going to last," I said to him one night. We were cuddling in bed. "You know that, don't you?"

"Yes," he replied. "But would you kiss me again just one more time?"

What could I do with this guy? Of course I kissed him, again and again. I was crazy about him.

We approached a year of dating. Nothing seemed to rock us. I still felt our relationship would end. I went to my therapist to find out how to move forward. She'd tell me the truth.

"Do you really love him?" my therapist asked with intensity in her voice.

"Yes," I said, "I do." I twisted a piece of Kleenex in my lap. "And I'm so afraid our affair can't last much longer. All the great things we do together will end. I can't bear the thought of losing him. I'd feel a deeper grief than I've ever felt before."

"Well," she said, looking directly at me, "if you love him, why don't you practice loving him every day?"

"Oh?" I said and drew back in my chair. "How am I supposed to love him every day?" I felt doubtful. What the hell was she talking about? My lousy track record with men haunted me. I wasn't sure how I'd be able to do daily loving. I'd never done it before.

She looked me square in the eye. We sat there in the room with that pregnant pause of silence between us. Then she leaned forward.

"Just do it," she said.

And I did—and I would—every single day since then.

36. FUNERALS

The phone rang just as John put our luggage outside the door. It was eleven at night. Who could be calling us at this hour? I picked up the phone. It was my sister in New York.

"Pop's in the hospital," she said. "Not sure what's going on, but it's probably his heart."

My mind went wild. We all knew about his heart condition and that he had been to the hospital months before. Did this trip mean he was in critical condition? In Greece, people think if you go to the hospital it means your death. I adored my father and hoped he would live long enough for me to visit Greece and see him one more time. *Please, Pop*, I thought, *please don't die on me now.*

We were waiting for the cab to take us to the airport to leave for New Zealand in just a few hours. Was my sister asking me to go to Greece? I didn't want to go to Greece. It was January and freezing there. *I love you Pop, so please hang on till I get back.* Incidentally, how the hell were we going to change our airline tickets on New Year's Eve to go to Greece? Too complicated. My emotions were running amok. There was no time to think of the right thing to do.

The rock-bottom truth was that I didn't want to hear my father's heart condition had sent him to some Athens hospital. I didn't want to hear he was sick and maybe dying. I didn't want to unpack my luggage to take out the bathing suit and shorts and put in heavy sweaters. I didn't want to travel umpteen hours by plane to get there. No way did I want to go to Greece.

There were other reasons I didn't want to change planes and plans, ones not easy to admit. John had just moved into my house, and the New Zealand trip was going to be like a honeymoon for us. We were going to a warm climate. This was our well-earned vacation. Selfishly, I wanted to be with my lover and play.

To add to the mix, I felt huge burnout from my job. Long hours as a therapist exhausted me. Great longing pulled me toward a warm getaway, a place to rest and relax. The trip was a reward for my hard work.

"We're leaving for New Zealand in a few hours," I said to my sister. "Here's our itinerary. We can't change our plans at this late hour. If you need to contact us and let us know what's going on, call. When we get back, we'll make plans to go to Athens and see Pop. Okay?"

I hung up the phone and looked at John. I loved this man very much. Could he sense the turmoil I felt at that moment? Of course I wanted to go away with him. We both needed this time away from our work. Yet, at the same time, love and obligation toward my father tore me to bits inside. He was the good guy, my mother the bad one. He favored me.

We'd seen my father in Greece the year before. I didn't want to make that trip again and spend it in a hospital. I couldn't do it.

John looked at me. He put his arms around me and held me close. "I know you love your father," he said, "but we can't go to Greece right now." He got it. He could see from my face, the tears filling my eyes. I wanted to see my father. I didn't want him to die, but couldn't make any decision at that moment. John looked away from me. "It's too late to change our plans." I didn't move. A full minute passed between us. "Come on," he said, pushing me toward the door. "Grab your luggage. We need to leave now."

The cab was waiting and took us to the airport. Neither of us spoke.

I could talk about our New Zealand trip, the scenery, the mountains, all about Fiji, and the interesting people we met. Like a robot, I brought my body there and saw many places. While I was functioning in a semi-normal way, my spirit was with my father in Athens, at his bedside at the hospital. My thoughts were with him all the time. I might as well have changed planes before we left. I wasn't in New Zealand at all.

When we got back home to California, I called my sister in New York. "Is Pop okay?" I asked.

"He died," my sister said. "I didn't want to spoil your vacation to tell you that."

I wept. I'd made the decision not to fly to Athens to see my father, and I felt great guilt about that decision. Why had I not changed plans as soon as we'd heard he was in the hospital? I did not feel strong enough to say to John, "I can't go to New Zealand. I have to go to Greece. This is my father and I love him. He may be gone when I get there, but I have to go anyhow." I regret I didn't say it.

My sister had flown to Athens and did not get to see my father in the hospital, but went to his funeral. She represented all of us who couldn't make it. "In his casket," she told me, "Pop looked good in a nice suit. Everyone was given a glass of Greek brandy. We took a sip and then threw the rest on

Pop." A farewell drink to toast his journey to the other world. I heard the Italian Mafia had a similar ritual when one of their mafiosi died.

My mind went to my mother where she lived in a retirement community in Astoria, she who cursed my alcoholic father daily and blamed him for her miserable life. "That rotten dog," she'd say. "May he rot in hell."

"Listen," I said to my sister. "Don't tell Momma Pop died." Despite our tumultuous past, I felt concerned for her. As a therapist, hadn't I heard many hateful relationship stories, only to learn beneath those emotions were deep feelings of love?

All my life I'd heard from my mother how terrible my father treated her, how he drank, gambled rent money away, and slept with other women. I suspected the other side of her hate for my father's misdeeds was love, and that underneath all that anger were deep tender feelings for him. This she could never admit to anyone. But I knew it. Much easier to rant and rave about his infidelities and abuses. To admit her love for him would have been impossible. Hatred for him kept her alive. In death she could no longer curse him.

"If you tell Mom," I told my sister, "she won't be able to handle it. She'll die too. Please don't tell her."

Long pause on the phone. "Too late," my sister said. "We did tell her."

———

Three months later, my mother died suddenly.

I missed my father's funeral in Athens, but I knew I wouldn't miss my mother's in New York. I had to go and say goodbye to her. Yes, I was angry. Her death hadn't given me enough time to grieve my father, and now I had to grieve them both. Since my mother could no longer curse my father,

I knew I could not follow in those footsteps and continue to blame her for my unhappiness. I needed to make some kind of peace with her.

When I arrived in New York and unpacked my luggage, I grabbed a cab to the funeral parlor. The relatives were there to honor her memory: the aunts, cousins, and my siblings sat there all looking solemn. I walked to the coffin to view my mother for the last time.

As I saw her lying in the coffin, looking peaceful and benign as though she were sleeping, an old fear gripped me. There was a familiar feeling of impending danger, the same one I felt as a young teen.

At any moment I expected her corpse to rise up, raise her hand, and strike me across the face for old time's sake, just so I would remember she still had control over me. Like a cobra ready to strike, she'd get her fangs clawing into me if I got too satisfied with my life and escaped her choking grip around my neck. Even in death, I still feared her. I believed she had powers beyond the grave to destroy me.

———

It wouldn't be until many years later, when I started writing about my mother, that I would see her character change from all dark and evil to something more nuanced. Before, I refused to see any good in her. But later I would see, in her provincial way, she influenced me more than I could admit. She haggled with all the local shopkeepers. I learned to bargain and discovered ways to negotiate everything just like my mother. She would make a meal from scraps in the refrigerator. At times I search the pantry before I cook, just as she did. I used to see people in my life as either good or bad. I would start to see other shades of their behavior as well. I could observe their other intentions, different indications of character. What my mother lacked in intellect, she made up in simple peasant wisdom and resourcefulness. I learned this from her.

Eventually I would release that victim part of me that insisted on dwelling on all the ways in which she wronged me. That doesn't mean it's gone for good. It's still there. But it doesn't take over my entire life, dominating every memory with unhappy gloom and sorrow. I am much more than what happened to me in my childhood.

ACKNOWLEDGMENTS

I am so thankful to Brooke Warner and She Writes Press for publishing my book.

To Katie Butler, who said, "I read the Tree story twice. I cried twice." Bless you for publishing my first piece in the *Psychotherapy Networker*. My therapists—Valerie H., Susan M., and especially the first one, Emily-Anne B.—a humble thanks for all you gave me. To my first creative writing teacher at L.A. City College, Izabelle Ziegler, who gave me A's on my papers, thank you. My writing teachers: Elizabeth Fishel, Mark Greenside, Louise Dunbar, Clive Matson, and the memoir class at the North Berkeley Senior Center. These classes had the most remarkable writers in them. They'd read my essays and give me the best feedback to go deeper and write better.

To Linda Joy Myers and Brooke Warner, who gave me the honor of being in their anthology, *The Magic of Memoir*. To my writing coaches—Linda Joy Myers, Charlotte Cook, and Kira Lynne Allen—thanks for believing in me when I didn't. Thanks for putting my feet to the fire to keep writing, especially when I resisted. Anne Fox, my beloved copy editor who reminds me to read my piece aloud, go over it carefully, and be patient.

To Nikki and the gang at TJ's—Nihal, Ed, Shelley, Dickie—I give thanks.

To my writing buddy, Karen Pliskin, thank you. She and I met years ago at Charlotte Cook's Creative Writing class at Piedmont Adult School. She'd read "The Tree" and said, "This is a good story. Send it out." Struggling with challenging pieces is hard. Having supportive company while I struggle makes the writing a bit easier. I'm grateful for that friendship.

To all my recovery family—Kathy, Bertha, David and everyone around the table—thanks.

To Liz, Bertha, Karen, Jane, and Anne—my beta readers—a big humble thanks.

To Heart and Soul Center of Light, Science of Mind Church in Oakland, I am on my knees with gratitude to the congregation, Rev. Andriette, Paulette, and my spiritual advisor, Bonnie Allen.

To my family, the New York one: my parents, Costa and Maria Fotopulos, my sisters, Titsa and Teddy, my brother, Bill, and all the nieces: Simone, Fran, Stephie, Valerie, Dawn, Madeline, and Denise. To Donna, Matt, and Jeff. Thank you for your support.

To the relatives in Greece: Photis, Bepsi, Mimi, Kiki, Stavros, and all the rest of the cousins from my mother's village in Plomarion—a humble thanks to all.

To my wonderful husband, John, what a guy. We're going on over thirty years, and I still love this man like crazy. You always believed in me.

God, I thank you for all your blessings—thank you, thank you, thank you.

ABOUT THE AUTHOR

Dr. Irene Sardanis is a retired psychologist. She was born in New York to Greek immigrant parents. She has been published five times in the *Sun Literary Magazine* and in many anthologies, the most recent of which was *The Magic of Memoir* in 2016. Dr. Sardanis attended writing conferences in San Miguel de Allende, Mexico; Key West, Florida; Mendocino, California; and Catamaran Writer's Conference at Pebble Beach, California. She's been invited to read from her memoir chapters on numerous occasions, in particular, "Carmen Miranda." She's attended writing classes and workshops with Elizabeth Fishel, Charlotte Cook, Mark Greenside, Elizabeth Rosner, Pam Huston, Clive Matson, Louise Dunbar, and Laura Davis. She occasionally moonlights as a jazz vocalist.

Dr. Sardanis resides in Oakland, California with her wonderful husband, John.

Author photo © Chris Loomis

SELECTED TITLES FROM SHE WRITES PRESS

She Writes Press is an independent publishing company founded to serve women writers everywhere. Visit us at www.shewritespress.com.

The S Word by Paolina Milana. $16.95, 978-1-63152-927-6. An insider's account of growing up with a schizophrenic mother, and the disastrous toll the illness—and her Sicilian Catholic family's code of secrecy—takes upon her young life.

Raising Myself: A Memoir of Neglect, Shame, and Growing Up Too Soon by Beverly Engel. $16.95, 978-1-63152-367-0. A powerfully inspiring and unflinchingly honest story of how best-selling author and abuse recovery expert Beverly Engel made her way in the world—in spite of her mother's neglect and constant criticism, undergoing sexual abuse at nine, and being raped at twelve.

Letting Go into Perfect Love: Discovering the Extraordinary After Abuse by Gwendolyn M. Plano. $16.95, 978-1-938314-74-2. After staying in an abusive marriage for twenty-five years, Gwen Plano finally broke free—and started down the long road toward healing.

Not Exactly Love: A Memoir by Betty Hafner. $16.95, 978-1-63152-149-2. At twenty-five Betty Hafner, thought she'd found the man to make her dream of a family and cozy home come true—but after they married, his rages turned the dream into a nightmare, and Betty had to decide: stay with the man she loved, or find a way to leave?

Lost in the Reflecting Pool: A Memoir by Diane Pomerantz. $16.95, 978-1-63152-268-0. A psychological story about Diane, a highly trained child psychologist, who falls in love with Charles, a brilliant and charming psychiatrist—ignoring all the red flags that will later come back to haunt her.

Baffled by Love: Stories of the Lasting Impact of Childhood Trauma Inflicted by Loved Ones by Laurie Kahn. $16.95, 978-1631522260. For three decades, Laurie Kahn has treated clients who were abused as children—people who were injured by someone who professed to love them. Here, she shares stories from her own rocky childhood along with those of her clients, weaving a textured tale of the all-too-human search for the "good kind of love."

www.ingramcontent.com/pod-product-compliance
Lightning Source LLC
Chambersburg PA
CBHW022250211224
19369CB00003B/51

9 781631 525391